MULTIDIMENSIONAL ITEM RESPONSE THEORY

Quantitative Applications in the Social Sciences

A SAGE PUBLICATIONS SERIES

1. Analysis of Variance, 2nd Edition *Iversen/Norpoth*
2. Operations Research Methods *Nagel/Neef*
3. Causal Modeling, 2nd Edition *Asher*
4. Tests of Significance *Henkel*
5. Cohort Analysis, 2nd Edition *Glenn*
6. Canonical Analysis and Factor Comparison *Levine*
7. Analysis of Nominal Data, 2nd Edition *Reynolds*
8. Analysis of Ordinal Data *Hildebrand/Laing/Rosenthal*
9. Time Series Analysis, 2nd Edition *Ostrom*
10. Ecological Inference *Langbein/Lichtman*
11. Multidimensional Scaling *Kruskal/Wish*
12. Analysis of Covariance *Wildt/Ahtola*
13. Introduction to Factor Analysis *Kim/Mueller*
14. Factor Analysis *Kim/Mueller*
15. Multiple Indicators *Sullivan/Feldman*
16. Exploratory Data Analysis *Hartwig/Dearing*
17. Reliability and Validity Assessment *Carmines/Zeller*
18. Analyzing Panel Data *Markus*
19. Discriminant Analysis *Klecka*
20. Log-Linear Models *Knoke/Burke*
21. Interrupted Time Series Analysis *McDowall/McCleary/Meidinger/Hay*
22. Applied Regression, 2nd Edition *Lewis-Beck/Lewis-Beck*
23. Research Designs *Spector*
24. Unidimensional Scaling *McIver/Carmines*
25. Magnitude Scaling *Lodge*
26. Multiattribute Evaluation *Edwards/Newman*
27. Dynamic Modeling *Huckfeldt/Kohfeld/Likens*
28. Network Analysis *Knoke/Kuklinski*
29. Interpreting and Using Regression *Achen*
30. Test Item Bias *Osterlind*
31. Mobility Tables *Hout*
32. Measures of Association *Liebetrau*
33. Confirmatory Factor Analysis *Long*
34. Covariance Structure Models *Long*
35. Introduction to Survey Sampling *Kalton*
36. Achievement Testing *Bejar*
37. Nonrecursive Causal Models *Berry*
38. Matrix Algebra *Namboodiri*
39. Introduction to Applied Demography *Rives/Serow*
40. Micro computer Methodsfor Social Scientists, 2nd Edition *Schrodt*
41. Game Theory *Zagare*
42. Using Published Data *Jacob*
43. Bayesian Statistical Inference *Iversen*
44. Cluster Analysis *Aldenderfer/Blashfield*
45. Linear Probability, Logit, and Probit Models *Aldrich/Nelson*
46. Event History and Survival Analysis, 2nd Edition *Allison*
47. Canonical Correlation Analysis *Thompson*
48. Models for Innovation Diffusion *Mahajan/Peterson*
49. Basic Content Analysis, 2nd Edition *Weber*
50. Multiple Regression in Practice *Berry/Feldman*
51. Stochastic Parameter Regression Models *Newbold/Bos*
52. Using Microcomputers in Research *Madron/Tate/Brookshire*
53. Secondary Analysis of Survey Data *Kiecolt/Nathan*
54. Multivariate Analysis of Variance *Bray/Maxwell*
55. The Logic of Causal Order *Davis*
56. Introduction to Linear Goal Programming *Ignizio*
57. Understanding Regression Analysis, 2nd Edition *Schroeder/Sjoquist/Stephan*
58. Randomized Response and Related Methods, 2nd Edition *Fox/Tracy*
59. Meta-Analysis *Wolf*
60. Linear Programming *Feiring*
61. Multiple Comparisons *Klockars/Sax*
62. Information Theory *Krippendorff*
63. Survey Questions *Converse/Presser*
64. Latent Class Analysis *McCutcheon*
65. Three-Way Scaling and Clustering *Arabie/Carroll/DeSarbo*
66. Q Methodology, 2nd Edition *McKeown/Thomas*
67. Analyzing Decision Making *Louviere*
68. Rasch Models for Measurement *Andrich*
69. Principal Components Analysis *Dunteman*
70. Pooled Time Series Analysis *Sayrs*
71. Analyzing Complex Survey Data, 2nd Edition *Lee/Forthofer*
72. Interaction Effects in Multiple Regression, 2nd Edition *Jaccard/Turrisi*
73. Under standing Significance Testing *Mohr*
74. Experimental Design and Analysis *Brown/Melamed*
75. Metric Scaling *Weller/Romney*
76. Longitudinal Research, 2nd Edition *Menard*
77. Expert Systems *Benfer/Brent/Furbee*
78. Data Theory and Dimensional Analysis *Jacoby*
79. Regression Diagnostics, 2nd Edition *Fox*
80. Computer-Assisted Interviewing *Saris*
81. Contextual Analysis *Iversen*
82. Summated Rating Scale Construction *Spector*
83. Central Tendency and Variability *Weisberg*
84. ANOVA: Repeated Measures *Girden*
85. Processing Data *Bourque/Clark*
86. Logit Modeling *DeMaris*
87. Analytic Mapping and Geographic Databases *Garson/Biggs*
88. Working With Archival Data *Elder/Pavalko/Clipp*
89. Multiple Comparison Procedures *Toothaker*
90. Nonparametric Statistics *Gibbons*
91. Nonparametric Measures of Association *Gibbons*
92. Understanding Regression Assumptions *Berry*
93. Regression With Dummy Variables *Hardy*
94. Loglinear Models With Latent Variables *Hagenaars*
95. Bootstrapping *Mooney/Duval*
96. Maximum Likelihood Estimation *Eliason*
97. Ordinal Log-Linear Models *Ishii-Kuntz*
98. Random Factors in ANOVA *Jackson/Brashers*
99. Univariate Tests for Time Series Models *Cromwell/Labys/Terraza*

Quantitative Applications in the Social Sciences

A SAGE PUBLICATIONS SERIES

100. Multivariate Tests for Time Series Models *Cromwell/Hannan/Labys/Terraza*
101. Interpreting Probability Models: Logit, Probit, and Other Generalized Linear Models *Liao*
102. Typologies and Taxonomies *Bailey*
103. Data Analysis: An Introduction *Lewis-Beck*
104. Multiple Attribute Decision Making *Yoon/Hwang*
105. Causal Analysis With Panel Data *Finkel*
106. Applied Logistic Regression Analysis, 2nd Edition *Menard*
107. Chaos and Catastrophe Theories *Brown*
108. Basic Math for Social Scientists: Concepts *Hagle*
109. Basic Math for Social Scientists: Problems and Solutions *Hagle*
110. Calculus *Iversen*
111. Regression Models: Censored, Sample Selected, or Truncated Data *Breen*
112. Tree Models of Similarity and Association *Corter*
113. Computational Modeling *Taber/Timpone*
114. LISREL Approaches to Interaction Effects in Multiple Regression *Jaccard/Wan*
115. Analyzing Repeated Surveys *Frebaugh*
116. Monte Carlo Simulation *Mooney*
117. Statistical Graphics for Univariate and Bivariate Data *Jacoby*
118. Interaction Effects in Factorial Analysis of Variance *Jaccard*
119. Odds Ratios in the Analysis of Contingency Tables *Rudas*
120. Statistical Graphics for Visualizing Multivariate Data *Jacoby*
121. Applied Correspondence Analysis *Clausen*
122. Game Theory Topics *fink/Gates/Humes*
123. Social Choice: Theory and Research *Johnson*
124. Neural Networks *Abdi/Valentin/Edelman*
125. Relating Statistics and Experimental Design: An Introduction *Levin*
126. Latent Class Scaling Analysis *Dayton*
127. Sorting Data: Collection and Analysis *Coxon*
128. Analyzing Documentary Accounts *Hodson*
129. Effect Size for ANOVA Designs *Cortina/Nouri*
130. Nonparametric Simple Regression: Smoothing Scatterplots *Fox*
131. Multiple and Generalized Nonparametric Regression *Fox*
132. Logistic Regression: A Primer *Pampel*
133. Translating Questionnaires and Other Research Instruments: Problems and Solutions *Behling/Law*
134. Generalized Linear Models: A Unified Approach, 2nd Edition *Gill/Torres*
135. Interaction Effects in Logistic Regression *Jaccard*
136. Missing Data *Allison*
137. Spline Regression Models *Marsh/Cormier*
138. Logit and Probit: Ordered and Multinomial Models *Borooah*
139. Correlation: Parametric and Nonparametric Measures *Chen/Popovich*
140. Confidence Intervals *Smithson*
141. Internet Data Collection *Best/Krueger*
142. Probability Theory *Rudas*
143. Multilevel Modeling, 2nd Edition *Luke*
144. Polytomous Item Response Theory Models *Ostini/Nering*
145. An Introduction to Generalized Linear Models *Dunteman/Ho*
146. Logistic Regression Models for Ordinal Response Variables *O'Connell*
147. Fuzzy Set Theory: Applications in the Social Sciences *Smithson/Verkuilen*
148. Multiple Time Series Models *Brandt/Williams*
149. Quantile Regression *Hao/Naiman*
150. Differential Equations: A Modeling Approach *Brown*
151. Graph Algebra: Mathematical Modeling With a Systems Approach *Brown*
152. Modern Methods for Robust Regression *Andersen*
153. Agent-Based Models, 2nd Edition *Gilbert*
154. Social Network Analysis, 3rd Edition *Knoke/Yang*
155. Spatial Regression Models, 2nd Edition *Ward/Gleditsch*
156. Mediation Analysis *Iacobucci*
157. Latent Growth Curve Modeling *Preacher/Wichman/MacCallum/Briggs*
158. Introduction to the Comparative Method With Boolean Algebra *Caramani*
159. A Mathematical Primer for Social Statistics *Fox*
160. Fixed Effects Regression Models *Allison*
161. Differential Item Functioning, 2nd Edition *Osterlind/Everson*
162. Quantitative Narrative Analysis *Franzosi*
163. Multiple Correspondence Analysis *LeRoux/Rouanet*
164. Association Models *Wong*
165. Fractal Analysis *Brown/Liebovitch*
166. Assessing Inequality *Hao/Naiman*
167. Graphical Models and the Multigraph Representation for Categorical Data *Khamis*
168. Nonrecursive Models *Paxton/Hipp/Marquart-Pyatt*
169. Ordinal Item Response Theory *Van Schuur*
170. Multivariate General Linear Models *Haase*
171. Methods of Randomization in Experimental Design *Alferes*
172. Heteroskedasticity in Regression *Kaufman*
173. An Introduction to Exponential Random Graph Modeling *Harris*
174. Introduction to Time Series Analysis *Pickup*
175. Factorial Survey Experiments *Auspurg/Hinz*
176. Introduction to Power Analysis: Two-Group Studies *Hedberg*
177. Linear Regression: A Mathematical Introduction *Gujarati*
178. Propensity Score Methods and Applications *Bai/Clark*
179. Multilevel Structural Equation Modeling *Silva/Bosancianu/Littvay*
180. Gathering Social Network Data *adams*
181. Generalized Linear Models for Bounded and Limited Quantitative Variables *Smithson/Shou*
182. Exploratory Factor Analysis *Finch*
183. Multidimensional Item Response Theory *Bonifay*

Sara Miller McCune founded SAGE Publishing in 1965 to support the dissemination of usable knowledge and educate a global community. SAGE publishes more than 1000 journals and over 800 new books each year, spanning a wide range of subject areas. Our growing selection of library products includes archives, data, case studies and video. SAGE remains majority owned by our founder and after her lifetime will become owned by a charitable trust that secures the company's continued independence.

Los Angeles | London | New Delhi | Singapore | Washington DC | Melbourne

MULTIDIMENSIONAL ITEM RESPONSE THEORY

Wes Bonifay

University of Missouri

Los Angeles | London | New Delhi
Singapore | Washington DC | Melbourne

FOR INFORMATION:

SAGE Publications, Inc.
2455 Teller Road
Thousand Oaks, California 91320
E-mail: order@sagepub.com

SAGE Publications Ltd.
1 Oliver's Yard
55 City Road
London, EC1Y 1SP
United Kingdom

SAGE Publications India Pvt. Ltd.
B 1/I 1 Mohan Cooperative Industrial Area
Mathura Road, New Delhi 110 044
India

SAGE Publications Asia-Pacific Pte. Ltd.
18 Cross Street #10–10/11/12
China Square Central
Singapore 048423

Printed in the United States of America

ISBN: 978-1-5063-8425-2

Acquisitions Editor: Helen Salmon
Content Development Editor: Chelsea Neve
Editorial Assistant: Megan O'Hefferman
Production Editor: Karen Wiley
Copy Editor: Liann Lech
Typesetter: Hurix Digital
Proofreader: Wendy Jo Dymond
Indexer: Naomi Linzer
Cover Designer: Candice Harman
Marketing Manager: Shari Countryman

This book is printed on acid-free paper.

MIX
Paper from responsible sources
FSC
www.fsc.org   FSC® C008955

19 20 21 22 23 10 9 8 7 6 5 4 3 2 1

CONTENTS

Series Editor's Introduction   ix

Acknowledgments   xi

About the Author   xiii

Chapter 1: Introduction   1

Chapter 2: Unidimensional Item Response Theory   5
    What Is a Latent Trait?   5
    Assumptions of UIRT   5
    UIRT Models for Dichotomous Data   6
    R Code   13
    UIRT Models for Polytomous Data   13
    Additional UIRT Models   17
    R Code   17
    UIRT Estimation   17
    Other Estimation Methods   26
    R Code   26

Chapter 3: MIRT Models for Dichotomous Data   27
    Compensation in MIRT Modeling   27
    Compensatory MIRT Models   31
    R Code   37
    Partially Compensatory MIRT Models   38
    R Code   41
    Additional MIRT Models for Dichotomous Data   41
    R Code   45
    Recent Advances in Dichotomous MIRT Modeling   45

Chapter 4: MIRT Models for Polytomous Data   47
    R Code   54
    Additional Polytomous MIRT Models   54

Chapter 5: Descriptive MIRT Statistics   55
    The θ-Space   55
    The Item Response Surface   57
    Conditional Response Functions   58
    The Direction of Measurement   60

Person Parameters in MIRT   67
MIRT Information   70
Polytomous MIRT Descriptives   71
Test-Level MIRT Descriptives   75

Chapter 6: Item Factor Structures   **77**
Two-Tier Model   77
Correlated-Traits Model   80
Bifactor Model   81
Testlet Response Model   81
R Code   82

Chapter 7: Estimation in MIRT Models   **83**
Conceptual Illustration   83
Missing Data Formulation   84
Two Challenges   87
Adaptive Quadrature   88
Bayesian Estimation   89
MH-RM Estimation   90
R Code   91

Chapter 8: MIRT Model Diagnostics and Evaluation   **93**
Dimensionality Assessment   93
Test-Level Fit Assessment   97
Item-Level Fit Assessment   100
Model Comparison Methods   103

Chapter 9: MIRT Applications   **105**
Linking and Equating   105
R Code   107
Differential Item Functioning   107
R Code   109
Computerized Adaptive Testing   109
R Code   111
Applications of the Two-Tier Item Factor Structure   111
Further MIRT Applications   113

References   **115**
Index   **133**

SERIES EDITOR'S INTRODUCTION

It is my pleasure to introduce *Multidimensional Item Response Theory*, by Wes Bonifay. Unidimensional item response theory (UIRT) is a statistical framework for the analysis of dichotomous (e.g., correct, incorrect) or polytomous (never, sometimes, always) test items that are assumed to measure a single construct. Multidimensional Item Response Theory (MIRT) extends UIRT to incorporate the possibility that answers to an item or test reflect more than one latent variable or construct. For example, reading ability may affect performance on a test designed to measure proficiency in mathematics. Initially developed in the context of educational testing, applications of MIRT are increasing in other arenas, for example, in the analysis of self-reports to measure anxiety, anger, and depression.

Multidimensional Item Response Theory is one of the more advanced volumes in the QASS Series. It is for readers already well grounded in UIRT and interested in expanding their knowledge and practice to include more complex models. For this group, Professor Bonifay provides an accessible, well explained, logical and carefully worked out introduction to MIRT. Throughout, UIRT serves as a foundation for launching discussions of describing, estimating, and evaluating MIRT models.

After a relatively brief but comprehensive review of UIRT in Chapter 2, Professor Bonifay introduces MIRT models by adding parameters to the UIRT model one at a time. The main focus of Chapter 3 is compensatory MIRT models, where, for example, either of two constructs might lead to a correct answer. Chapter 3 also introduces partially compensatory models, variable compensation models, diagnostic classification models, and, in Chapter 4, MIRT models for polytomous data. Chapter 5 takes up item- and test-level descriptives such as the multidimensional difficulty and discrimination indices; for this chapter, readers might want to brush up on their trigonometry. Chapter 6 discusses item factor structures, including the two-tier model, the testlet model, and the bifactor model. Estimation is the focus of Chapter 7. Multidimensionality complicates the estimation process, and efficient approaches have only been developed recently. In this chapter, Professor Bonifay provides a general overview of MIRT estimation methods (e.g., adaptive quadrature, Bayesian, and Metropolis-Hastings Robbins-Monro approaches), and points interested readers to advanced resources. Diagnostics are addressed in Chapter 8. These include dimensionality assessment, test- and item-level fit assessment, and model comparisons. The final chapter concludes with some applications under development right now.

A hallmark of the volume is the extensive use of graphical displays. These visualizations are essential to the pedagogy as they provide intuition as to the logic underlying various models and procedures. The graphics are helpful in the discussion of UIRT models, for example, illustrating the parameters (discrimination, difficulty, guessing, and inattention) and the consequences of each for the item response functions and information functions. The graphics are critical to the discussion of MIRT models, as here, we are operating in multidimensional space. Professor Bonifay pairs item response surfaces and contour plots in a way that is extraordinarily useful in illustrating the various MIRT models and clarifying differences between them.

In addition to a well-organized introduction to MIRT models, the volume provides several resources that will be helpful to readers. First, Professor Bonifay has created a Companion Student Study Site at **study.sagepub.com/researchmethods/qass/bonifay-multidimensional-item-response-theory-1e** that illustrates the procedures and applications discussed in the volume. The Companion Student Study Site leverages a second resource, a freely available *irtDemo* package developed by Professor Bonifay and a collaborator for the R statistical software environment (Bulus & Bonifay, 2016). Between the two, readers will be able to replicate most of the visualizations in the volume as well as some that cannot be rendered in print, such as the animation of a 360-degree rotating 3-dimensional response surface! Third, the text points to published examples that illustrate the kinds of models and issues discussed in the text. Fourth, basic R programming syntax is included throughout the text to enable readers to conduct their own MIRT analyses. As mentioned, this is an advanced text, but for readers with the appropriate background, it pulls together, organizes, presents the technical literature in an accessible way, and, in doing so, will increase the use of MIRT models in social science generally as well as in educational psychology and evaluation.

—*Barbara Entwisle*

Series Editor

ACKNOWLEDGMENTS

The author would like to acknowledge Dr. Steve Reise and Dr. Li Cai, whose mentorship and instruction contributed substantially to this volume. I am especially grateful to QASS Series Editor Barbara Entwisle for her valuable suggestions and advice, and to SAGE Senior Acquisitions Editor Helen Salmon for her assistance and support. Most important, thank you to Julie for her never-ending patience and encouragement.

Dedicated to my daughter, Wren, who will be disappointed to learn that I did not fulfill her request for a chapter on how to draw animals.

The author and SAGE would like to thank the following reviewers for their feedback:

Maria Pampaka, The University of Manchester
Yan Yan Sheng, Southern Illinois University
Gustavo Gonzalez-Cuevas, Idaho State University

ABOUT THE AUTHOR

Wes Bonifay is Assistant Professor in the Statistics, Measurement, and Evaluation in Education program in the College of Education at the University of Missouri. He earned his PhD in Quantitative Psychology from the University of California, Los Angeles in 2015. His research focuses on the development, evaluation, and application of multidimensional item response theory and other latent variable measurement models. His work has appeared in journals such as *Multivariate Behavioral Research* and *Structural Equation Modeling*.

Chapter 1

INTRODUCTION

In any statistical modeling scenario, whether the model represents atoms or galaxies or the human brain, it is essential that all variables are measured with optimal precision. Without exact and meticulous measurement, the model may not be an accurate representation of the real-world phenomena under investigation. In the field of psychometrics, the variables in the model are psychological in nature—academic proficiency, personality traits, severity of psychiatric symptoms, and so on. Psychological constructs such as these are inherently complicated and multifaceted, and relatively simple models that only measure a single construct are often insufficient approximations of complex data. As Zhang (2007) noted, "the unidimensionality of a set of items usually cannot be met and most tests are actually multidimensional to some extent" (p. 69). Accordingly, several decades of psychometric research have led to the development of sophisticated models for multidimensional test data, and in recent years, multidimensional item response theory (MIRT) has become a burgeoning topic in psychological and educational measurement. With regard to theoretical development, MIRT is the focus of ongoing research by many leading quantitative methodologists, who are continually supplying the psychometric community with novel and innovative statistical techniques. In terms of application, MIRT has been successfully implemented not only in psychology and education but also in economics, biostatistics, psychiatry, and a number of other scientific disciplines that demand precise measurement of multidimensional psychological constructs.

MIRT is rightly considered to be a cutting-edge statistical technique; indeed, the methodology underlying MIRT can become exceedingly complex, and many leading psychometricians and researchers are actively building upon the foundations of MIRT in increasingly sophisticated ways. As a result, this topic may not receive much attention in an introductory item response theory (IRT) course. In this author's opinion, however, it is a major misperception to regard MIRT as too advanced or intimidating for inexpert audiences. While MIRT offers many technical challenges, it can certainly be understood and applied by readers who have a firm grounding in unidimensional IRT modeling. As with other titles in the Quantitative Applications in the Social Sciences (QASS) series, the purpose of the book is to present the foundations of an advanced quantitative topic in a palatable and concise format to students, instructors, and researchers. It includes many practical examples and illustrations, along with numerous intuitive and informative figures and diagrams. In addition, many high-quality applied MIRT research articles are cited and discussed throughout the text to demonstrate how the various models and methods are being used in the real world. A particularly useful accompaniment to this volume is the freely available irtDemo package (Bulus & Bonifay, 2016) for the R statistical software environment (R Core Team, 2018). This package was specifically designed to provide students and other learners with a hands-on approach to IRT modeling via a suite of interactive applets. By using these applets, readers can easily manipulate and inspect the complex output produced by several common MIRT models and gain a greater understanding of potentially difficult topics. Furthermore, the irtDemo package can be used to create MIRT figures for use in academic publications; in fact, many of the figures presented in this book were created using irtDemo. This package can be downloaded from the Comprehensive R Archive Network at **https://cran.r-project.org/package=irtDemo**.

In addition, brief snippets of R code are interspersed throughout the text (with the complete R code included on the Companion Student Study Site at **study.sagepub.com/researchmethods/qass/bonifay-multidimensional-item-response-theory-1e**) to guide readers in exploring MIRT models, estimating the model parameters, generating plots, and implementing the various procedures and applications discussed throughout this book. The R code is primarily based on the mirt package (Chalmers, 2012), which provides a powerful, flexible toolkit for advanced psychometric modeling. With the hands-on interactive irtDemo applet and the implementable R code, readers will be well equipped to conduct MIRT analyses, interpret results, communicate findings, and even provide instruction in this advanced statistical topic.[1]

Finally, it is important to note that this book, like many titles in the QASS series, is more of an overview of an advanced statistical method than a technical reference source. In an effort to present MIRT methods and models in a palatable and usable format, the rigorous mathematical underpinnings of MIRT are not discussed herein. If you require derivations and proofs, then you may find a volume such as Baker and Kim (2004) more beneficial.

This book is structured as follows: Chapter 2 offers a brief review of unidimensional IRT (UIRT), covering data assumptions, dichotomous and polytomous UIRT models, descriptive statistics, and UIRT parameter

---

[1] A thorough and user-friendly guide to IRT in R is offered by Desjardins and Bulut (2018). Also, readers who are less familiar with R should note that many of the models and methods discussed in this volume can be implemented in general statistical software like Mplus (L. Muthén & Muthén, 2017), SAS (SAS Institute Inc., 2015), and SPSS (via the SPIRIT macro; DiTrapani, Rockwood, & Jeon, 2018).

estimation. Each of the sections in Chapter 2 includes only the essential details with limited exposition regarding the finer points of IRT. The goal is to refresh your memory of unidimensional IRT models and methods in preparation for the subsequent chapters on MIRT.

Chapters 3 and 4 expand upon the common UIRT measurement models to include multiple latent traits. Chapter 3 presents MIRT models for dichotomous response data, whereas Chapter 4 focuses on polytomous MIRT models. After describing the testing scenarios in which these models are appropriate, each of these chapters then presents the relevant equations along with numerous visualizations and interpretations of these models and their parameters. Readers should note that this book offers limited information on multidimensional Rasch models. Interested readers may consult Briggs and Wilson (2003) for an introduction to multidimensional Rasch modeling.

Chapter 5 covers several ways of describing the results of a MIRT analysis. One of the many challenges in understanding MIRT models is how to make sense of the parameter estimates and other statistical properties of multidimensional items/tests. This chapter presents both item- and test-level descriptives, including multidimensional item response surfaces, information functions, and other important components of standard MIRT output.

Chapter 6 explores several common MIRT factor structures. These structures describe the overall arrangement of the latent variables, their connections to one another, and their relationships with the item responses. This chapter focuses primarily on a recent development in MIRT modeling: the flexible two-tier item factor analysis model, which encompasses a number of simpler item factor structures, including the popular bifactor model.

Chapter 7 presents several methods of estimating the parameters in the MIRT models discussed in Chapters 3 through 5. This chapter introduces the estimation complications that arise due to the presence of multiple latent traits and then reviews three contemporary techniques of estimating the MIRT model parameters.

Chapter 8 focuses on an important component of any statistical modeling endeavor: the diagnosis and evaluation of the model. This chapter details several MIRT model diagnostics, including dimensionality assessment, test-level goodness of fit, and the evaluation of item-level fit. This chapter will provide you with the tools to carefully appraise the quality of a MIRT model and thereby uncover its strengths and/or shortcomings.

Finally, Chapter 9 presents several informative and cutting-edge applications of MIRT. This chapter presents a handful of the many exciting MIRT applications that have been developed in recent years, including large-scale assessment analysis, longitudinal modeling, linking and equating, differential item functioning, and computerized adaptive testing.

Chapter 2

UNIDIMENSIONAL ITEM RESPONSE THEORY

This chapter a brief review of unidimensional aimed at readers who are already familiar with the topic. The goal of this chapter is to refresh your memory of unidimensional IRT models and methods in preparation for the following chapters on MIRT. Each of the sections in this chapter includes only the essential details, with limited technical discussion. References for further reading are included throughout, though most IRT texts (e.g., de Ayala, 2009; Embretson & Reise, 2000; Thissen & Wainer, 2001) offer in-depth coverage of the topics discussed in the following.

What Is a Latent Trait?

IRT is a statistical framework for the measurement of psychological variables, which are commonly referred to as constructs, attributes, or traits. Examples of such traits include intelligence, mathematical proficiency, political ideology, impulsivity, and countless other attitudes, abilities, propensities, or disorders. Because such variables cannot be directly observed, they are often described as *latent traits*; they exist only in the mind of an individual and are latent, or hidden, until they manifest in some observable behavior. In the context of psychological or educational assessment, that observable behavior is the pattern of responses to test *items* (i.e., the questions, prompts, or other stimuli on a test). Through the use of measurement models—such as IRT, factor analytic, or latent class models—we are able to link the latent trait(s) to the observed behavior and thereby measure the level (i.e., the amount, degree, or severity) of the psychological variable(s) in each respondent.

Assumptions of UIRT

The appropriate application of an IRT model requires that the data meet three assumptions: unidimensionality, local independence, and monotonicity. If the data satisfy all three of these assumptions, UIRT may be an appropriate analytical tool for your research purposes. If any of these assumptions are violated, then a more complex, perhaps multidimensional IRT model will be necessary to counteract the violated assumption(s).

Unidimensionality is the assumption that the items are interrelated due to the presence of a single latent trait underlying the item responses. For

5

example, a biology quiz would be unidimensional if differences among the responses to the item stimuli can be sufficiently accounted for by differences in a single factor, such as scientific knowledge. If the responses are also influenced by some secondary factor, say, reading proficiency, such that beyond any differences in scientific knowledge, students with advanced reading skills are outperforming students with rudimentary reading skills, then the quiz is no longer measuring a single latent trait. In this case, the assumption of unidimensionality would be violated, and a typical UIRT model would no longer be an appropriate method of analysis.

A closely related IRT assumption is local independence, which holds that after accounting for a single dimension, there are no residual dependencies (i.e., leftover connections) among the items. In other words, the assumption of local independence says that test items should be related only to a single common factor, and beyond that common factor, there should not be any significant correlations remaining. If the assumption of local independence is violated to a nonignorable degree, then UIRT will not suffice and you should consider applying a multidimensional approach that will allow you to directly model the residual dependencies between items.

The final assumption is that of monotonicity, which holds that the probability of a correct response or endorsement increases as respondents' locations along the latent trait become higher. For instance, an item on the biology quiz would be monotonic if respondents of low scientific knowledge have a low probability of responding correctly and that this probability increases as knowledge increases. Violations of the monotonicity assumption often indicate an item that has been reverse-worded but not reverse-coded in the data. Usually, such violations can simply be corrected by inspecting the data.

UIRT Models for Dichotomous Data

In order to provide a brief overview of dichotomous IRT models, we focus on a general formulation, as its parameters can be constrained to produce the most widely used dichotomous models. The 4-parameter logistic (4PL) IRT model (Barton & Lord, 1981) is given by

$$P\left(x_{ip} = 1 \mid \theta_p; a_i, b_i, g_i, u_i\right) = g_i + \left(u_i - g_i\right)\frac{\exp[a_i(\theta_p - b_i)]}{1 + \exp[a_i(\theta_p - b_i)]}, \quad (2.1)$$

where the probability P of a correct response $x = 1$ on item i by person p is conditioned on the ability θ of person p and four parameters of item i. These four parameters are a (the item's discrimination parameter, which quantifies the degree to which it successfully differentiates between individuals of low and high abilities); *b* (the item's difficulty parameter); *g* (the nonzero lower asymptote, or "guessing," parameter associated with correct responses at the extreme low end of the θ scale); and *u* (the upper asymptote, or "inattention," parameter associated with incorrect responses at the extreme high end of the θ scale).

Note that the parameters in Equation (2.1) can be constrained in various ways to produce the common dichotomous IRT models. When u_i, the upper asymptote parameter, is fixed at 1.0, then Equation (2.1) reduces to the popular 3-parameter logistic (3PL) model (Birnbaum, 1968). If we also set the "guessing" parameter g_i to 0.0, then Equation (2.1) becomes a 2-parameter (2PL) model, where items are described only in terms of discrimination and difficulty. If we then constrain the discrimination parameter a_i to 1.0, we arrive at the most parsimonious IRT model—the so-called Rasch model (Rasch, 1960)—wherein item difficulty is the sole parameter of interest.

The preceding explanation presents the exponent of the UIRT model in Equation (2.1) in terms of a_i (discrimination) and b_i (difficulty). However, it is also useful to consider an alternate way to parameterize the UIRT model. The slope-intercept parameterization is found by rearranging the exponent by distributing the a_i term, such that $a_i(\theta_p - b_i) = a_i\theta_p - a_ib_i$. If we relabel the term $-a_ib_i$ as c_i, then the exponent become $a_i\theta_p + c_i$, which is the familiar expression for a straight line. This parameterization places the model in the context of linear regression, where a_i represents the slope of the (logit) regression line and c_i represents the intercept. Note that the intercept term does not offer the easy interpretation of the difficulty parameter; however, if you have obtained results from a slope-intercept model and wish to interpret the parameters in terms of item difficulty, you can apply the simple transformation $b_i = c_i/a_i$.

Before we discuss these models and parameters further, we will also review the concept of item information in UIRT. *Information* is a statistical term meaning reduction in uncertainty. In IRT, and psychometrics in general, the parameter that we want to be most certain about is θ—the respondent's true ability or, more precisely, the respondent's true location along the latent trait continuum. The models described earlier provide $\hat{\theta}$—an estimate of the true location—but that estimate will be an uncertain approximation of the truth. We want to reduce this uncertainty by administering items that provide the most information about the true location. The 4PL item information function (IIF), as formulated by Magis (2013), is denoted by

$$I(\theta) = \frac{a_i^2 \left(P(\theta) - g_i\right)^2 \left(u_i - P(\theta)\right)^2}{\left(u_i - g_i\right)^2 P(\theta)\left(1 - P(\theta)\right)}, \tag{2.2}$$

where $P(\theta)$ is the 4PL model presented in Equation (2.1). The particular values of $I(\theta)$ are usually not interpreted, but the peak of this function, and its dispersion around that peak, is indicative of the most informative range of the θ scale (i.e., the region of ability for which a given item yields the most precise measurement). Note that, as with Equation (2.1), the 4PL IIF shown in Equation (2.2) will reduce to more familiar (2PL, 3PL) IIF forms by constraining the g_i and/or u_i parameters accordingly.

Figure 2.1 illustrates the role of the discrimination parameter a_i in defining the shape of the IIF and the item response function (IRF), that is, the mathematical function that relates the latent trait to the probability of a correct response. In the plot on the left, we see three IRFs, which represent three different relationships between the latent trait θ along the x-axis and the probability of a correct response $P(x = 1|\theta)$ along the y-axis. Each IRF presents a different degree of discrimination, as noted in the legend, while the three remaining parameters are fixed at particular values (the g and u parameters have been set to 0 and 1, respectively, resulting in the well-known 2PL function). The dotted curve represents the most highly discriminating item ($a_i = 2.5$), which has the steepest slope; the dashed curve represents a moderately discriminating item ($a_i = 1.0$); and the solid curve represents a weakly discriminating item ($a_i = 0.5$) and thus has the mildest slope.

The concept of discrimination can be understood by comparing the correct response probability of each IRF at a given range of θ. Consider, for instance, locations along the x-axis ranging from -1 to $+1$. For the most highly discriminating (dotted curve) item, a person located at $\theta = -1$ has around a .01 probability of providing a correct answer, while someone located at $\theta = +1$ has about a .99 probability of correct response. That is, the difference between these two respondents is quite stark; if a respondent answers this dotted item correctly, then we can be fairly confident that he or she has above-average ability. For the weakest (solid curve) item, however, a person located at $\theta = -1$ has around a .30 probability of correct response, while someone located at $\theta = +1$ only has a .70 probability of correct response. The solid curve (which is, in fact, a Rasch model because $a = 1.0$) is therefore less successful at differentiating these two individuals; if a respondent answers the solid item correctly, we can be somewhat confident that he or she has above-average ability, but there is still a nonignorable .30 probability associated with a low ability.

The right panel of Figure 2.1 displays the information function associated with each of the IRFs in the left panel. Clearly, a more discriminating IRF, as represented by the dotted curve, will provide much more information about a test-taker's true location along the θ continuum. In contrast, the solid curve, which has a weak discrimination parameter of $a = 0.5$, is

Figure 2.1 Item response functions (left) and information functions (right) of three 4PL item response functions with parameters $b = 0$, $g = 0$, $u = 1$, and varying discrimination (a) parameters.

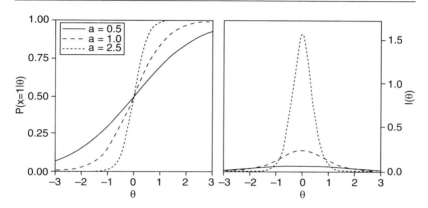

basically flat when plotted on the same axes as the other IIFs, while the solid item is wholly uninformative.

In the previous figure, the difficulty parameter b was fixed at zero, which explains why all three IRFs intersect at the coordinates ($\theta = 0$, $P = 0.50$). In Figure 2.2, the difficulty parameter varies from −1 to +1, while the discrimination parameter a is fixed at 1.0. Difficulty in IRT is defined relative to the inflection point of the IRF (i.e., the point on the function at which the curve changes direction). In dichotomous IRT models, item difficulty is represented by the x-coordinate of the inflection point. In the 2PL model, where the lower asymptote is equal to 0 and the upper asymptote is equal to 1, the y-coordinate of the inflection point is at precisely $P = 0.50$. The arrows in Figure 2.2 serve as visual aids for understanding item difficulty. The horizontal arrows cross through the inflection points of each IRF and meet the y-axis at $P = 0.50$, while the vertical arrows extend from the inflection points of each IRF to the θ axis, thereby indicating the difficulty of each response function. In less mathematical terms, the difficulty parameter of the 2PL model represents the point on the latent trait scale at which there is a 0.50 probability of correct response. If the examinee's proficiency or ability is higher (or lower) than this point, then he or she will have a higher (or lower) than 0.50 probability of answering correctly.

Item difficulty also plays a role in the location of the information function. The right panel of Figure 2.2 presents the IIFs that correspond to the IRFs in the left panel. The peaks are identical because the discrimination parameters

10

Figure 2.2   Item response functions (left) and information functions (right) of three 4PL item response functions with parameters $a = 1$, $g = 0$, $u = 1$, and varying difficulty (b) parameters.

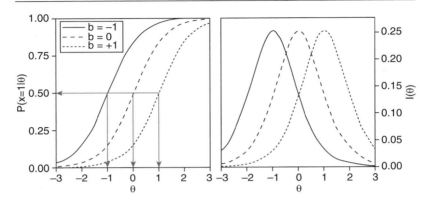

are fixed at 1; here (as in all Rasch models), information only varies according to item difficulty. Thus, the solid curve provides the most accurate measurement of true locations for persons of below-average ability (around $\theta = -1$), while the dashed and dotted curves indicate heightened measurement precision around $\theta = 0$ and $+1$, respectively. In other words, the item represented by the solid curve will help to identify true θ values (i.e., reduce the uncertainty about $\hat{\theta}$) at the low range of ability, but it will not provide much information regarding the true θ values of respondents at the high end of the scale.

The lower and upper asymptotes of the item response function can also be adjusted from 0 and 1, respectively. A nonzero lower asymptote indicates that among persons located at the extreme low end of the θ scale, the probability of correct response is greater than zero. Thus, the lower asymptote parameter is commonly referred to as the "guessing" (or, more accurately, "pseudo-guessing") parameter and is labeled accordingly here as g. The idea is that respondents of extremely low ability may be able to guess the correct answer, perhaps by choosing among the available options on a multiple-choice exam. The effect of such guessing is an artificially elevated θ estimate; because the respondent guessed correctly, his or her ability appears to be higher than it truly is. Birnbaum (1968) introduced the 3-parameter logistic (3PL) model to account for such response bias and thereby obtain more precise estimates of true θ locations.

Figure 2.3 displays three examples of 3PL functions. Here, the a and b parameters discussed earlier are fixed at 1 and 0, respectively, while the g parameter varies. When $g = 0$ (the solid curve), the 3PL function reduces to a 2PL. As g increases, the lower asymptote moves further up the y-axis, thereby reflecting the nonzero probability of correct response among persons of extremely low ability. On a 5-point multiple-choice question, for example, we may expect to see a "guessing" probability of $P = 1/5$ (or 0.20), as reflected by the dashed response function in Figure 2.3. An important detail regarding interpretation of the 3PL is that the difficulty parameter is no longer associated with $P = 0.50$. The dashed curve, for example, has a lower asymptote at $P = 0.40$, so setting the difficulty parameter at $P = 0.50$ does not make much sense. Instead, we retain the original interpretation: Item difficulty is the x-coordinate of the inflection point of the IRF.

Though it may be too subtle to notice in the panel on the left, the inflection point of each 3PL function changes as the lower asymptote increases. We can see this shift, however, in the information plot on the right, because the peak of an information function occurs at the inflection point of the logistic response function. The vertical lines are included as a visualization of this shift. The solid line reflects the $g = 0.0$ model, where the inflection point is at exactly $b = 0$. When g increases to 0.2 or 0.4, the inflection point shifts slightly to the right, as indicated by the dashed and dotted lines. Furthermore, the height and skewness of the information function is altered as g goes up. Thus, the effect of the lower asymptote parameter is that it reduces the amount of information *and* shifts the location of most precise measurement to the right. This may seem like a technical nuance, but it reflects common sense: A correct guess does not give us any useful information about the true ability of individuals who are located at the low end of the latent trait continuum.

Figure 2.3 Item response functions (left) and information functions (right) of three 4PL item response functions with parameters $a = 1$, $b = 0$, $u = 1$, and varying lower asymptote (g) parameters.

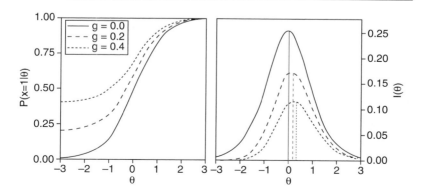

12

Finally, let us consider *u*—the upper asymptote parameter of the 4PL logistic function. This parameter allows for a non-1.0 upper asymptote, meaning that persons located at the extreme high end of the θ scale may answer incorrectly. Such decreased probabilities are sometimes explained as the result of inattention on the part of the respondent or some clerical error on the part of the test developer. A non-1.0 probability may also reflect an extraordinarily difficult item, such as an item about suicidal intent on a depression questionnaire. In this case, the theoretically true asymptote may be 1.0, but for a practical range of depression (say, –3 to +3), *P* may be less than 1.0 even among the highest θ values. Barton and Lord (1981) developed the 4PL model with the same aim as the 3PL: to improve estimation of the person location parameter θ. Their reasoning was that failure to account for consistent errors among persons with high abilities would lead to downward bias when estimating θ (i.e., $\hat{\theta}$ will be lower when *u* = 1 than when *u* < 1). That is, the true θ location of such respondents will appear to be lower than it actually is.

Figure 2.4 visualizes the 4PL model by fixing parameters *a*, *b*, and *g* and only allowing *u* to vary. You may have noticed that this figure actually displays 3 parameters (*a*, *b*, and *u*) rather than 4, because *g* is constrained to zero. Such a model is sometimes referred to as a 3PLu model (e.g., in the mirt R package) because it estimates the upper rather than lower asymptote. In a true 4PL model, both the upper and lower asymptotes would deviate from 1 and 0, respectively. In the panel on the right, we see how modifications to *u* affect the information function: As the *u* parameter deviates from

Figure 2.4 Item response functions (left) and information functions (right) of three 4PL item response functions with parameters *a* = 1, *b* = 0, *g* = 0, and varying upper asymptote (*u*) parameters.

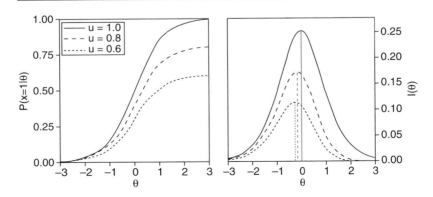

1.0, the item becomes less informative (lower peaks) and the inflection point (and thus the point of most precise measurement) shifts slightly to the left.

It is worth noting that, in addition to introducing the 4PL model, Barton and Lord (1981) also studied its utility. Based on simulation results, they determined that the 4PL did not offer substantial improvements in θ estimation, concluding that "there is no compelling reason to urge the use of this model" (p. 6). However, the 4PL is presented here because the more useful and widely used dichotomous IRT models (2PL and 3PL) are easily derived from the 4PL formulation in Equation (2.1).

R Code

In the mirt package (Chalmers, 2012), the basic IRT modeling syntax is

```
output <- mirt(data = mydata, model = mymodel),
```

where `mydata` represents the categorical item response data that you wish to analyze, and `mymodel` indicates the item factor structure (see Chapter 6 of this volume). In the unidimensional (i.e., 1-factor) case, `mymodel` should be set to 1. The argument itemtype can be added to the `mirt()` command to specify each of the dichotomous UIRT models presented earlier (e.g., itemtype = 'Rasch', '2PL', '3PL', or '4PL'). The mirt package also allows estimation of the inverted 3PL (itemtype = '3PLu'). After estimating your chosen model, the parameter estimates can be viewed using `coef(output)`, item response functions can be plotted using `itemplot(output, item = itemnumber)`, and many other results can be obtained. See the mirt help documentation for more details.

UIRT Models for Polytomous Data

We turn now to UIRT models for data that are scored in more than two categories. Polytomous response data are produced by items with ordinal response scales (e.g., Likert-type self-report items, partial credit test items) and nominal response scales. When there are more than two categories, there may not be a "correct" response probability, so the goal is typically to identify the probability of responding in a particular category k (e.g., the probability of selecting *Strongly Agree* on a Likert-type item), given the respondent's location along the latent trait scale. The various polytomous response models fall into two classes: difference models and divide-by-total models (Thissen & Steinberg, 1986).

Difference Models

Difference models begin by defining the cumulative probabilities $P_k^* = P\left(x_{ip} \geq k \mid \theta_p\right)$ among the response options. For example, the probability of responding in a category $k \geq 0$, denoted P_0^*, is exactly 1.0 because any observed response necessarily must be in category 0 or higher. The probability P_1^* of responding in category $k \geq 1$ is then estimated from the response data. Taking the difference between P_0^* and P_1^* leaves category $k = 0$ in isolation. In the same manner, we can model the response function of each category. This class of models includes the graded response model (GRM) and its various extensions.

Samejima (1969) developed the GRM by applying the principles of traditional dichotomous UIRT models to the polytomous data case. Specifically, the GRM treats a multiple-category response scale as a series of dichotomies. For example, a Likert scale from 0 = *Strongly Disagree* to 3 = *Strongly Agree* can be split such that a response of $k = 0$ defines one response grouping and responses of $k = \{1, 2, \text{ or } 3\}$ define a second grouping. This transforms the polytomous response scale into a 0 versus 1+ dichotomy; similar splits are made among the remaining response options. The GRM then models $P\left(x_{ip} = k \mid \theta_p\right)$, the probability of selecting response option k on item i, given the location of person p along the θ scale, by taking the difference $P_{ik}^* - P_{ik+1}^*$, where

$$P_{ik}^* = P\left(x_{ip} \geq k\right) = \frac{\exp[a_i(\theta_p - b_k)]}{1 + \exp[a_i(\theta_p - b_k)]}. \tag{2.3}$$

The right side of Equation (2.3) indicates that each dichotomy is fit with the standard 2PL model described earlier. In the GRM, these "category boundary curves" differ in terms of location (i.e., the b_k parameters vary for each category k) but are constrained to have equal discrimination (i.e., the a_i parameter is the same for all categories within item i). By definition, the lowest response category P_{i0}^* is 1.0, because the probability that the response x_{ip} is greater than or equal to $k = 0$ is necessarily 1.0. Differences are then taken between the adjacent category boundary curves that remain. The information function for the difference class of polytomous UIRT models is found by summing the information across all m response categories of item i:

$$I_i\left(\theta\right) = \sum_{k=0}^{K} P_{ik}\left(\theta\right) a_i^2 \left\{ P_{ik}^*\left(\theta\right)\left[1 - P_{ik}^*\left(\theta\right)\right] + P_{i,k+1}^*\left(\theta\right)[1 - P_{i,k+1}^*\left(\theta\right)] \right\}. \tag{2.4}$$

The GRM is perhaps best understood through graphical representation. Figure 2.5 displays the category response functions of a 3-category item and its information function. Each curve on the left is associated with a particular response option. Thus, the probability of selecting the lowest category ($k = 0$, the solid line) is highest when respondents are located at the extreme low end of the θ scale and lowest when respondents are located at the extreme high end. The opposite relationship holds for the probability of selecting the highest category ($k = 2$, the dotted line). The probability of selecting the middle category ($k = 1$, the dashed line) is highest when the respondent is located near the middle of the latent trait continuum. Notice that for any given θ location, the category response probabilities sum to 1.0.

As the right panel of Figure 2.5 shows, the information function in a polytomous model may be multimodal. Here, the information function has two peaks: The most precise estimates of θ occur when the respondent is located around -1 or $+1$, which happens to be where the category response functions intersect.

Divide-by-Total Models

An alternative class of polytomous UIRT models is known as the divide-by-total class (Thissen & Steinberg, 1986). In such models, rather than taking the difference between adjacent category boundary curves, the response probability is found by dividing some positive category response

Figure 2.5 Category response functions (left) and information function (right) of a graded response model with parameters $a = 1$, $b_1 = -1$, and $b_2 = 1$.

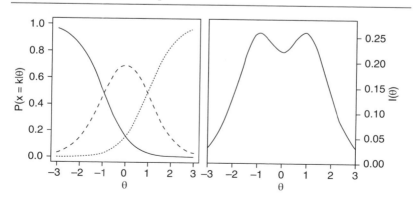

function $z_{ik}(\theta)$ by $\sum_{h=1}^{m_i} z_{ih}(\theta)$, the sum of all m category response functions.

For instance, in the nominal response model (NRM; Bock, 1972), $z_{ik} = \exp(a_k\theta_p + c_k)$, such that the probability of selecting category k is given by

$$P\left(x_{ip} = k \mid \theta_p; \mathbf{a}_i, \mathbf{c}_i\right) = \frac{\exp\left(a_k\theta_p + c_k\right)}{\sum_i \exp\left(\mathbf{a}_i\theta_p + \mathbf{c}_i\right)}. \tag{2.5}$$

Here, $\mathbf{a}_i$ is a vector of discrimination parameters $a_1, a_2, \ldots, a_k$ and $\mathbf{c}_i$ is a vector of intercepts $c_1, c_2, \ldots, c_k$, as presented in the slope-intercept parameterization discussed earlier. For the model to work properly, one of the response categories must be specified (possibly arbitrarily) as a reference category; all parameters associated with this reference category are then fixed to zero. Furthermore, Bock specified that all a_ks and c_ks must sum to zero, as accomplished by a transformation matrix of deviation contrasts, in order to identify the model. This results in unique response probabilities, with different discrimination and difficulty parameters, for each category.

The NRM can be used when the response options have no meaningful numeric order. The most straightforward application of the NRM is in analyzing data from certain nominal survey items in which the response options are a list with no a priori ordering (e.g., selecting a political affiliation). Another common application involves fitting the NRM to data from a multiple-choice item to determine the θ location that is associated with each incorrect distractor choice. This model is also the most general form of the divide-by-total class of UIRT models. If the discrimination parameters in vector $\mathbf{a}_i$ are constrained to equality, then Equation (2.5) becomes the (generalized) partial credit model (Muraki, 1992). If all discrimination parameters are further constrained to be equal to exactly 1.0, then Equation (2.5) is the partial credit model (Masters, 1982). The NRM also encompasses the (generalized) rating scale model (Andrich, 1978). The information function for the divide-by-total class of polytomous UIRT models is

$$I_i\left(\theta\right) = \sum_{k=0}^{K} \left[\frac{P'_{ik}\left(\theta\right)^2}{P_{ik}\left(\theta\right)} - P''_{ik}\left(\theta\right)\right], \tag{2.6}$$

where $P'_{ik}\left(\theta\right)$ and $P''_{ik}\left(\theta\right)$ are the first and second derivatives of $P_{ik}\left(\theta\right)$ (see Magis, 2015, for details).

Additional UIRT Models

Aside from the common dichotomous and polytomous models presented in this chapter, there are a number of specialized UIRT models that are intended for use with certain data types or in alignment with particular psychometric theories. Additional models include unfolding models, in which agree-disagree or similar response formats are modeled according to an ideal point process rather than a cumulative response probability (Roberts, Donoghue, & Laughlin, 2000; Roberts & Laughlin, 1996); unipolar models, which focus on the measurement of latent traits with scales that conceptually cannot fall below zero (e.g., addiction, gambling; Lucke, 2014, 2015); polynomial models, which allow for complex item response functions that deviate from the traditional logistic/ogive form (Falk & Cai, 2016b, 2016c); models with asymmetric item response functions (S. Lee & Bolt, 2017, 2018); and nonparametric models, in which item response data are modeled without specifying some family of parametric functions (e.g., normal ogive, logistic; Sijtsma & Molenaar, 2002), among many alternatives. Several of these models, along with others that have been underutilized in the IRT literature, can be applied using the sirt package (Robitzsch, 2019) in R.

R Code

To conduct a polytomous UIRT analysis, you simply modify the `item-type` argument within the `mirt()` command presented earlier. The mirt package supports `itemtype = 'graded'`, `'gpcm'`, `'nominal'` for the GRM, the generalized partial credit model (GPCM), and the NRM, respectively, as well as several less common UIRT models.

UIRT Estimation

Until now, our discussion has presumed that the item and person parameters in each UIRT model are known. In practice, however, these parameters are not known and must be estimated from the observed patterns of responses to the test items under investigation. To introduce the concept of estimation in UIRT, we will focus on Darrell, a student who has taken a chemistry exam. Our goal is to estimate Darrell's location along a single latent trait continuum (i.e., knowledge of chemistry). For now, we will continue to treat the item parameters as known.

Suppose that Darrell was able to respond correctly to the first item on the exam, which has a difficulty parameter of $b = 0.5$. By coding correct answers as 1 and incorrect answers as 0, we can notate Darrell's response pattern thus far: [1]. That is, he provided a correct response to the first item. What is our best guess about Darrell's knowledge of chemistry after administering one item? It is most likely that, because he responded correctly, Darrell's knowledge is greater than the difficulty of the first item (i.e., $\theta > 0.5$; though it is possible that Darrell's knowledge is actually below the difficulty parameter [i.e., $\theta < 0.5$] and he just got lucky). At this point, we have an indeterminate estimate: After one item, we can only estimate whether Darrell's location is above (or below) the difficulty parameter of the item, but we cannot determine his exact placement along the θ scale.

Suppose that the second item on Darrell's test is harder than the first, with a previously calibrated difficulty parameter of $b = 1.0$. Darrell responds incorrectly to this item, resulting in a response pattern of [10] for Items 1 and 2, respectively, thereby providing important information regarding our estimate of his knowledge of chemistry. We now know that his knowledge is likely located somewhere between the difficulty of the first item, which he was able to answer correctly, and the difficulty of the second item, which he failed to answer correctly. In other words, $0.5 < \theta < 1.0$. (Notice that if Darrell had answered Item 2 correctly, then we would still have an indeterminate estimate. Our best guess would be that his knowledge is somewhere above 1.0, but it could be anywhere from slightly above 1.0 to $+\infty$.)

Each item on the chemistry exam is scored dichotomously as correct or incorrect, meaning we can fit each item with the constrained 2PL version of the general dichotomous IRT function presented earlier. For simplicity, and with a bit of altered notation, here is Equation (2.1) with the lower asymptote (g_i) parameter fixed at 0.0 and the upper asymptote (u_i) parameter fixed at 1.0:

$$P_i\left(\theta_p; a_i, b_i\right) = \frac{\exp\left[a_i(\theta_p - b_i)\right]}{1 + \exp\left[a_i(\theta_p - b_i)\right]}. \tag{2.7}$$

This equation represents the probability P_i of correct response to a particular item i. To make this formulation more general, such that it addresses both correct and incorrect responses, we will define X_{ip} as a Bernoulli-distributed random variable representing person p's response to item i and x_{ip} as the observed (0-1) response. Then the conditional probability of $X_{ip} = x_{ip}$ is

$$P_i\left(X_{ip} = x_{ip} \mid \theta_p; a_i, b_i\right) = \left[P_i\left(\theta_p; a_i, b_i\right)\right]^{x_{ip}} \left[1 - P_i\left(\theta_p; a_i, b_i\right)\right]^{1-x_{ip}}. \tag{2.8}$$

On the right side of this equation, $P_i(.)$ represents the probability of a correct response (a monotonically increasing item response function), and $1 - P_i(.)$ is the probability of an incorrect response (which has a monotonically decreasing item response function and is sometimes denoted $Q_i(.)$). The exponential terms in Equation (2.8) indicate whether person p provided a correct response to the particular item i. If person p responded correctly, then $x_{ip} = 1$ and the second exponent becomes $1 - x_{ip} = 0$, causing the term $[1 - P_i(.)]$ to drop out of the equation. If person p responds incorrectly, then $x_{ip} = 0$ and the term $P_i(.)$ drops out of the equation instead. In other words, a correct response isolates the first term on the right side of Equation (2.8), such that the item response function reflects the probability of a correct response, while an incorrect response isolates the second term on the right side of Equation (2.8), such that the item response function represents the probability of an incorrect response.

Equations (2.7) and (2.8) refer to the response probability of a single item, but as we saw in Darrell's case, multiple item responses are needed if we are to obtain a precise estimate of θ. Recall the unidimensionality assumption of UIRT, which holds that a single latent trait is the sole source of covariation among the item responses. More specifically, this assumption implies an important statistical property known as *conditional independence*: The response probabilities across multiple items are independent for each respondent, conditional on his or her location along the single latent trait θ. Conditional independence enables us to multiply individual item response probabilities and thus determine the likelihood of a *pattern* of responses $X_p = (x_{1p}, x_{2p}, \ldots, x_{1p})$:

$$L(X_p \mid \theta_p; \gamma_i) = \prod_{i=1}^{I} \left[P_i\left(\theta_p; a_i, b_i\right) \right]^{x_{ip}} \left[1 - P_i\left(\theta_p; a_i, b_i\right) \right]^{1-x_{ip}}, \qquad (2.9)$$

where the vector γ_i contains all of the item parameters (i.e., in the 2PL case, the a and b parameters of every item in pattern X_p). The likelihood function produced by Equation (2.9) will be an inverted parabola whose peak represents the precise θ location that is most likely to produce the observed response pattern X_p.

In practice, we focus on the natural logarithm of the likelihood:

$$\log L(X_p \mid \theta_p; \gamma_i) = \sum_{i=1}^{I} x_{ip} \log\left[P_i\left(\theta_p; a_i, b_i\right) \right] \\ + \left(1 - x_{ip}\right) \log\left[1 - P_i\left(\theta_p; a_i, b_i\right) \right]. \qquad (2.10)$$

We refer to this function as the observed data log-likelihood and its peak as the maximum likelihood estimate (MLE). With regard to computation, the log-likelihood is more convenient than the likelihood because it is a sum instead of a product. Yet it will provide the same result, because the maximum of the log-likelihood function is located at the same θ coordinate as the likelihood itself.

The relationship between the item properties and the log-likelihood function is shown in Figure 2.6. Here, the item response functions represent the probabilities of responding correctly (and incorrectly) to five dichotomous chemistry items. The left panel of Figure 2.6 shows the log-likelihood associated with response pattern $X_p = [11000]$—the first pair (i.e., the two easiest items) were answered correctly, and the last three were answered incorrectly. The height of the likelihood function is the MLE, which, in the case of UIRT, represents the θ estimate that is most likely to produce this response pattern; it appears to be somewhere around –0.5. The right panel illustrates a respondent with greater knowledge of chemistry: The response pattern $X_p = [11110]$ appears to be most likely when θ is just below 2.

We can get a more precise estimate of the most likely θ value by plugging the item parameters into the log-likelihood function in Equation (2.10). We will focus on response pattern $X_p = [11000]$, which indicates that the log-likelihood function will use $P_i(.)$ for the first two items and $1 - P_i(.)$ for the last three. Suppose that these items were fit with a Rasch model (i.e.,

Figure 2.6 Log-likelihood functions of two different response patterns to a five-item test with difficulty parameters $b = \{-2, -1, 0, 1, 2\}$.

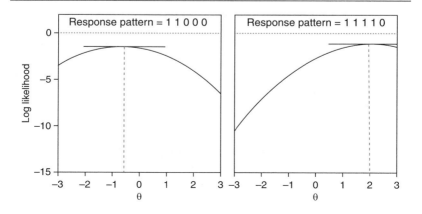

$P_i(\cdot) = \dfrac{\exp(\theta-b)}{1+\exp(\theta-b)})$ with difficulty parameters $b = [-2, -1, 0, 1, 2]$. Thus, the log-likelihood is

$$
\begin{aligned}
\log L(11000 \mid \theta_p) = \log &\left[\frac{\exp(\theta-(-2))}{1+\exp(\theta-(-2))}\right] + \log\left[\frac{\exp(\theta-(-1))}{1+\exp(\theta-(-1))}\right] \\
&+ \log\left[1 - \frac{\exp(\theta)}{1+\exp(\theta)}\right] + \log\left[1 - \frac{\exp(\theta-1)}{1+\exp(\theta-1)}\right] \quad (2.11) \\
&+ \log\left[1 - \frac{\exp(\theta-2)}{1+\exp(\theta-2)}\right].
\end{aligned}
$$

If we plug our crude guess of $\theta = -0.5$ into each log term in this equation, then $L(11000 \mid \theta = -0.5) = (-.202) + (-.475) + (-.473) + (-.201) + (-.079) = -1.430$. However, if we substitute a guess of $\theta = -0.6$, then $L(11000 \mid \theta = -0.5) = -1.426$. Our second guess is greater than the first, which means -0.6 is closer to the peak of the function and thus a slightly more likely estimate of θ. To find the precise maximum of the likelihood function (i.e., the MLE), we would need to use calculus-based optimization techniques such as the Newton-Raphson algorithm (see de Ayala, 2009, Embretson & Reise, 2000, or Thissen & Wainer, 2001, for further details on the Newton-Raphson algorithm). By computing the first derivative (also known as the *gradient*) of the log-likelihood and setting it to zero, we will find that the precise MLE is located at $\theta = -0.591$, where the height of the log-likelihood is -1.426. In summary, the MLE tells us that the examinee who produced response pattern $\mathbf{X}_p = [11000]$ is most likely to be located at $-.591$ on the θ scale.

Joint Estimation of Both Person and Item Parameters

So far, we have demonstrated how a precise estimate of θ can be found by locating the peak of the log-likelihood function relative to a particular response pattern $\mathbf{X}_p$. The same reasoning could be applied to estimate the most likely item parameters (e.g., the a and b parameters of the 2PL model). A more efficient approach, however, is to estimate the person and item parameters simultaneously. The key to this approach was introduced by Bock and Lieberman (1970), who removed the effect of individual person parameters by treating the θ values as a random sample from a population distribution. By integrating over that distribution, the item parameters can then be estimated relative to the marginal distribution of θ; this approach is therefore known as marginal maximum likelihood (MML) estimation (see Hartwell, Baker, & Zwarts, 1988, for an accessible overview of this topic).

In the 2PL case, the joint probability of the observed response pattern X_p and the latent variable θ, given the item parameters in γ_i, is the product of the likelihood times the prior probability of θ:

$$P\left(X_p, \theta; \gamma\right) = \prod_{i=1}^{I} \left[P_i\left(\theta; a_i, b_i\right)\right]^{x_{ip}} \left[1 - P_i\left(\theta; a_i, b_i\right)\right]^{1-x_{ip}} h(\theta). \qquad (2.12)$$

The term $h(\theta)$ (also known as the Bayesian *prior* distribution) represents one's beliefs about the distribution of θ in the population; $h(\theta)$ is therefore prespecified by the researcher and has no freely estimated parameters. A common UIRT specification, which is also the default in many software programs, is that $h(\theta)$ is normally distributed with a mean of 0 and a standard deviation of 1. The marginal probability of response pattern X_p, given the item parameters in γ, can then be found by integrating out the person parameter θ:

$$P\left(X_p; \gamma\right) = \int \prod_{i=1}^{I} \left[P_i\left(\theta; a_i, b_i\right)\right]^{x_{ip}} \left[1 - P_i\left(\theta; a_i, b_i\right)\right]^{1-x_{ip}} h(\theta) d\theta. \qquad (2.13)$$

We now have all the components we need to apply Bayes' theorem (Bayes, 1763) and obtain the *posterior* distribution of the person parameter θ. When applied to IRT estimation, Bayes' theorem holds that the posterior distribution is our best guess about an examinee's location after specifying our prior expectations about θ and calculating the likelihood based on the examinee's item response pattern:

$$P\left(\theta \mid X_p; \gamma\right) = \frac{P\left(X_p, \theta; \gamma\right)}{P\left(X_p; \gamma\right)}, \qquad (2.14)$$

where the numerator is the joint probability in Equation (2.12) and the denominator is the marginal probability in Equation (2.13). Unfortunately, after all this work, we have run into a complex mathematical obstacle: The integral in the marginal probability means that the posterior cannot be computed analytically. Fortunately, Bock and Aitkin (1981) developed a clever way to bypass this roadblock.

The EM Algorithm

Bock and Aitkin (1981) demonstrated that the integral in the marginal probability (i.e., the denominator of Equation [2.14]) can be precisely approximated by dividing the θ range into a set of rectangles whose heights correspond to the shape of the integral; summing these rectangles will produce a usable approximation of the area under the curve. This method is called Gauss-Hermite quadrature (or numerical integration); quadrature points are the demarcations along the x-axis that correspond to the width of the rectangles. In UIRT estimation, the intractable marginal probability in the posterior distribution can be approximated by specifying a set of J quadrature points and summing over them:

$$P\left(X_{p};\gamma\right) \approx \sum_{j=1}^{J}\prod_{i=1}^{I}\left[P_{i}\left(q_{j};a_{i},b_{i}\right)\right]^{x_{ip}}\left[1-P_{i}\left(q_{j};a_{i},b_{i}\right)\right]^{1-x_{ip}} w_{j}, \qquad (2.15)$$

where q_{j} represents a quadrature point. Quadrature rules are specified by the user and should cover the mass of the probability distribution with a manageable degree of granularity. For example, the mirt package in R specifies, by default, 61 quadrature points ranging from –6 to +6 (i.e., in intervals of 0.2; Chalmers, 2012). The height of the probability distribution at each point q_{j} is represented by the quadrature weight w_{q}, which corresponds to the prior distribution $h(.)$ such that $w_{q} = h\left(q_{j}\right) / \sum_{j=1}^{J} h\left(q_{j}\right)$. Bock and Aitkin (1981) also demonstrated how quadrature can be used to approximate the posterior distribution.

Finally, we arrive at the conditional expected complete data log-likelihood:

$$\begin{aligned} Q\left(\gamma \mid \mathbf{X};\gamma^{*}\right) \approx \sum_{i=1}^{I}\sum_{j=1}^{J} & r_{ij} \log\left[P_{i}\left(q_{j};a_{i},b_{i}\right)\right] \\ & +\left(n_{ij}-r_{ij}\right)\log\left[1-P_{i}\left(q_{j};a_{i},b_{i}\right)\right], \end{aligned} \qquad (2.16)$$

where n_{ij} is the expected number of persons at quadrature point j and r_{ij} is the conditional expected proportion of persons at that point who responded correctly to item i. In UIRT estimation, this is the log-likelihood function that we wish to maximize, thereby obtaining estimates of all item parameters in the model.

To ensure that these estimates are stable, the components are implemented by utilizing the expectation-maximization (EM) algorithm (Dempster, Laird, & Rubin, 1977), which works in the following manner. In the E-step, provisional parameter estimates $\gamma^{(k)}$ (user-specified or default starting values in the first iteration) are used to evaluate $Q(\gamma|\mathbf{X}; \gamma^{*})$. More specifically, the unobserved θ values that contribute to the complete data log-likelihood are replaced with their conditional expectations, and integration across θ is sidestepped through the use of quadrature. In the M-step, the maximum of the complete data log-likelihood is determined using ordinary estimation methods. This will yield an updated set of item parameter estimates $\gamma^{(k+1)}$, which are the most likely estimates given the provisional estimates $\gamma^{(k)}$. The updated estimates are then passed back to the E-step and the algorithm cycles through as many EM iterations as necessary to reach convergence. In most estimation situations, convergence is achieved when the difference between the estimates from adjacent cycles is below some threshold (e.g., the default tolerance for E-step convergence in the mirt package is .0001; Chalmers, 2012).

Scoring

Implementation of MML and the EM algorithm will provide estimates of the item parameters but not the person locations. In IRT, the task of estimating the location of an examinee along the θ scale is known as scoring. There are two main scoring methods in IRT, both of which are based on the posterior distribution produced by the Bayes formula (Equation [2.14]). Expected a posteriori (EAP) scores are found by computing the mean of the posterior distribution, while maximum a posteriori (MAP) scores are found by determining the maximum of the posterior distribution. EAPs are more commonly reported than MAPs because it is easier to find the mean than to determine the maximum; identifying the precise maximum of the posterior requires iterative optimization methods that are computationally intensive. However, an EAP score may not be as accurate a representation of the posterior distribution, especially if the posterior deviates considerably from normality.

These scoring methods are visualized in Figure 2.7. Notice that the middle two panels depict the same response pattern $X_p = [11000]$ that we examined earlier, though here we see the likelihood rather than the log-likelihood (as we saw earlier, the [log-]likelihood of this pattern peaks at $\theta = -.591$). The top panel displays the prior, which reflects our belief that chemistry knowledge is normally distributed in the population, and the bottom panel displays the posterior, which shows our updated guess as to the θ location associated with response pattern X_p. However, our prior distribution suggests that we should give less weight to this estimate, since it deviates slightly from our belief that knowledge of chemistry follows a normal distribution with mean 0. Accordingly, both the EAP and MAP scoring methods strike a compromise between the prior and log-likelihood, and our updated estimate is $\theta = -.27$. Interested readers can use the irtDemo package in R (Bulus & Bonifay, 2016) to explore the relationships between the shape of the prior distribution and the response pattern and their effects on the EAP and MAP estimates.

Figure 2.7 Bayesian scoring of a five-item test with a normal prior, item difficulty parameters $b = \{-2, -1, 0, 1, 2\}$, and response pattern = 1 1 0 0 0.

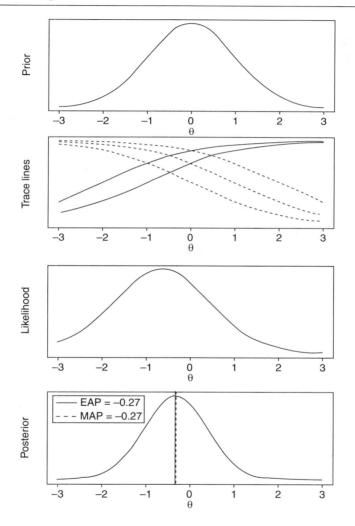

Finally, it is worth noting that specification of a prior distribution also addresses an advantage of MML over ordinary maximum likelihood (ML) estimation of item response data. While ML estimation is often useful and straightforward, test data present a challenge. Consider the situation in which an examinee responds correctly to all items on the science exam (i.e., $X_p = [11111]$). If we plug this pattern into Equation (2.19), we will find that the likelihood function increases infinitely as θ increases, meaning there is no MLE. This indeterminate result is common sense: If an examinee is able to answer every item correctly, then we only know that his or her location along the latent trait continuum is somewhere beyond the highest value in our θ range. The same problem occurs at the low end of the θ range when the response pattern $X_p = [00000]$. By incorporating statistical information about the low and high ends of the latent trait in the prior distribution $h(\theta)$, MML will facilitate estimation of these all-or-none response patterns. The normal prior presented earlier, for example, reflects the belief that, in the population, extremely high (or low) locations are relatively rare. Thus, multiplying the likelihood by the prior (as in Equation [2.10]) will result in a posterior density from which EAPs and MAPs can be computed.

Other Estimation Methods

It is worth noting that MML is not the only viable approach to parameter estimation in UIRT modeling. The item difficulty parameter in the Rasch model, for instance, can be estimated using conditional ML or joint ML (see Linacre, 1999). As an alternative to ML-based techniques, one could also implement Bayesian methods such as Markov chain Monte Carlo simulation, a method discussed in the context of multidimensionality in Chapter 7 of this text.

R Code

EM is the default estimation method in the mirt package, though a number of alternatives can be implemented by inserting the method argument within the `mirt()` command. After fitting an IRT model as described earlier, the EAP or MAP scores can then be obtained via fscores (output, method = 'EAP' or 'MAP').

Chapter 3

MIRT MODELS FOR DICHOTOMOUS DATA

In Chapter 2, we discussed several UIRT models that are designed to measure an examinee's location along a single latent trait continuum. MIRT models, as the name indicates, involve multiple latent traits. Let us begin our exploration of MIRT modeling by considering the following example, in which Allan, a second-grade student, is presented with a test item:

Item 1: A cheetah sprinted 1.5 kilometers in the morning and rested until the afternoon. In the evening, the cheetah then took a 500-meter stroll to the watering hole. How far did the cheetah travel in total?

On the surface, this item appears to be a standard mathematics word problem designed to measure Allan's proficiency in addition. Suppose, however, that the probability of responding correctly to Item 1 depends on more than one latent trait. Perhaps a high probability of correct response involves proficiency in several math skills. Maybe there are different problem-solving strategies that will lead, either independently or in some combination, to a correct response. Fortunately, MIRT provides many models that will allow us to better understand the latent traits underlying the probability of a correct response. To introduce MIRT modeling, we will assume that Item 1 is scored dichotomously (as correct or incorrect) and that the latent traits associated with this item align to the standard 2PL response function we reviewed in the previous chapter. Before presenting our first MIRT model, however, we must discuss the concept of compensation.

Compensation in MIRT Modeling

MIRT models can be broadly classified according to how the latent traits interact. A compensatory MIRT model is one in which high proficiency on one latent trait can compensate for low proficiency on the other trait(s). In a partially compensatory MIRT model, high proficiency on one latent trait will not compensate for low proficiency on the other(s); in other words, the probability of a correct response is high only if the examinee is proficient with regard to *all* traits being measured by the item.

Consider Item 1 from earlier. Perhaps you are interested in measuring problem-solving strategies and you wish to examine two different tactics that could be used to arrive at the correct answer to Item 1. For example,

Allan may use standard computation (θ_{com}), adding 1.5 km + 500 m to arrive at the proper solution. A second strategy might involve visualization (θ_{vis})—drawing a diagram or number line to represent the distance traveled by the cheetah. Either of these strategies will suffice on its own. That is, Allan is likely to respond correctly if he is proficient in computation, even if he is a poor illustrator. Conversely, he is likely to respond correctly if he excels at visualization, even if he is less skilled in computation. Furthermore, if Allan is competent in *both* strategies, it is highly likely that he will provide the correct response. In this example, θ_{com} and θ_{vis} could be represented by a compensatory MIRT model in which proficiency in one strategy will compensate for a deficiency in the other strategy.

Compensatory items are said to involve disjunctive component processes (Maris, 1999). In logic and mathematics, the key operator in disjunctive reasoning is the term *or*: the logical statement "A or B" is true if either A *or* B (or both) is true. If we translate this into MIRT terms, we see that a correct response is expected if Allan is proficient in θ_{com} or in θ_{vis} or in both θ_{com} and θ_{vis}. This scenario is depicted in Figure 3.1. Here, the diagonal line

Figure 3.1 Hypothetical compensatory combinations of proficiency in computation (θ_{com}) and visualization (θ_{vis}) that are associated with a $P = 0.5$ of responding correctly to Item 1.

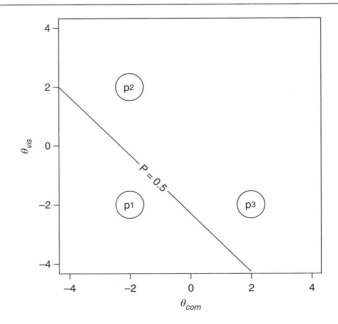

represents the hypothetical combinations of θ_{com} and θ_{vis} that are associated with a .50 probability of a correct response. Examinees whose combined proficiencies are located to the left of this line have a less than .50 probability of responding correctly, and those to the right have a greater than .50 probability of correct response. The person located at circle p_1 in this contrived figure is unlikely to respond correctly due to deficiencies in both strategies ($\theta_{com} = -2$; $\theta_{vis} = -2$). However, person p_2 is likely to give a correct response, because high ability in visualization ($\theta_{vis} = 2$) will compensate for low computation skills ($\theta_{com} = -2$). Similarly, person p_3 is expected to respond correctly because of computational proficiency ($\theta_{com} = 2$) despite a subpar ability to visualize the solution ($\theta_{vis} = -2$).

Maybe you are interested in assessing certain academic skills rather than problem-solving strategies. To provide a correct answer to Item 1, it is clear that the respondent must be able to read the problem *and* perform the required mathematical operations. If Allan does not know the words *sprinted, kilometer, meter,* or *stroll,* for example, then this will affect his ability to correctly answer this item. He must also have the mathematical ability to convert meters to kilometers (or vice versa) and add the two terms together to arrive at the correct sum. In IRT terms, the probability of a correct response to this item is then conditional on two latent traits: reading ability (θ_{read}) and math ability (θ_{math}). If you believe that experts in reading will be likely to provide a correct response even if they are terrible at math (or vice versa), then a compensatory MIRT model, as described earlier, could be applied. On the other hand, a partially compensatory[1] model should be used if you believe that excellent reading ability will not necessarily lead to a correct response if Allan is lacking in the necessary math skills (or, conversely, that being a math whiz will not necessarily allow Allan to answer correctly if he struggles to read the problem).

Partially compensatory items involve conjunctive component processes (Maris, 1999). The key operator in conjunctive reasoning is the term *and*, meaning the logical statement "A and B" is true only if A is true *and* B is true. Translated to MIRT terms, this statement says that a correct response is expected only if the examinee is proficient (to some degree) in θ_{read} *and* in θ_{math}. This situation is depicted in Figure 3.2, where the curve represents the combinations of abilities that are associated with a 0.5 probability of

---

[1] Many IRT researchers use the term *partially compensatory* interchangeably with *noncompensatory*. In this author's opinion, the label *noncompensatory* is a misnomer, as it implies in absolute terms that one ability will never compensate for another; in fact, such models are partially compensatory because there are regions of the multidimensional latent trait space in which compensation occurs and regions in which it does not (DeMars, 2016; see Figure 3.2).

Figure 3.2 Hypothetical partially compensatory combinations of proficiency in reading (θ_{read}) and math (θ_{math}) that are associated with a $P = 0.5$ of responding correctly to Item 1.

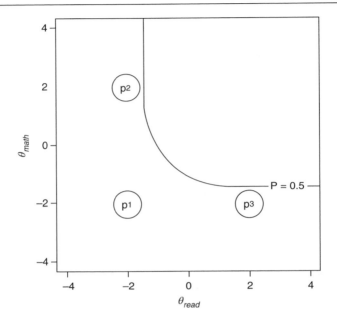

correct response. Here, persons p_1, p_2, and p_3 are placed at the same locations as in the previous example. Person p_1 is still not expected to provide a correct response because of low proficiency in both reading and math ($\theta_{read} = -2$; $\theta_{math} = -2$). Person p_2 is now expected to answer incorrectly because examinees with low reading ability ($\theta_{read} < -1.5$) are never expected to provide the right answer, no matter how high their math ability may be. Likewise, person p_3 is likely to respond incorrectly because examinees with inadequate proficiency in math ($\theta_{math} < -2.0$) are not expected to provide the right answer, no matter how outstanding their reading skills may be. In other words, the partially compensatory relationship between the latent traits requires that an individual possess some degree of proficiency in both math and reading ($\theta_{read} > -1.5$ *and* $\theta_{math} > -1.5$) in order to respond correctly.

Most MIRT applications use compensatory models, as they retain the interpretability of the simpler UIRT models that we reviewed in the previous chapter. Partially compensatory models are less common and somewhat more complicated in terms of both the statistics underlying the models and, especially, interpretation of the results. Thus, our MIRT modeling discussion begins with compensatory formulations. (We will assume, for now, that all parameter values are known; the statistical estimation of these parameters are discussed in Chapter 7.)

Compensatory MIRT Models

Just as in UIRT, MIRT models can be applied to data from dichotomous (true/false, correct/incorrect, agree/disagree) response scales. Although these response options may be limited, the MIRT models that can handle these types of data cover a range of complexity. We will begin our exploration of compensatory MIRT models by extending the most well-known dichotomous UIRT models.

Multidimensional 2-parameter logistic model. Our first MIRT model is an extension of the unidimensional 2PL model that was discussed in the previous chapter. The multidimensional 2-parameter logistic (M2PL) model[2] is given by

$$P\left(x_{ip} = 1 \mid \boldsymbol{\theta}_p ; \mathbf{a}_i, c_i\right) = \frac{\exp\left[\left(\sum_{m=1}^{M} a_{im}\theta_{pm}\right) + c_i\right]}{1 + \exp\left[\left(\sum_{m=1}^{M} a_{im}\theta_{pm}\right) + c_i\right]}. \tag{3.1}$$

Here, the a, θ, and c parameters retain their UIRT meanings (i.e., discrimination, ability, and intercept, respectively), but the sigma notation indicates that the M2PL response function is found by summing over the latent dimensions $m = 1, 2, \ldots, M$. We can rewrite Equation (3.1) using matrix notation, wherein the bolded terms represent a *vector* of multiple values, as opposed to the nonbolded *scalars* (i.e., single values) that we used in the UIRT formulations of the previous chapter:

$$P\left(x_{ip} = 1 \mid \boldsymbol{\theta}_p ; \mathbf{a}_i, c_i\right) = \frac{\exp\left(\mathbf{a}_i \boldsymbol{\theta}'_p + c_i\right)}{1 + \exp\left(\mathbf{a}_i \boldsymbol{\theta}'_p + c_i\right)}. \tag{3.2}$$

Thus, the M2PL provides the probability P of a correct response $x_{ip} = 1$ to item i by person p, given that person's vector of abilities $\boldsymbol{\theta}_p$, the vector of item discrimination parameters $\mathbf{a}_i$, and the intercept term c_i. The first vector

---

[2] As you may have expected, the M2PL can also be represented as a normal ogive model rather than a logistic model. See McDonald (1997) for further information.

in Equation (3.2) that we will consider is θ_p, which denotes the multiple θ latent traits believed to underlie the probability of correct response. The subscript p indicates that θ is a *person* parameter. In our example Item 1, θ_p is the vector $\{\theta_{com}, \theta_{vis}\}$ because a correct response is contingent on test-taker p's ability to compute (θ_{com}) and/or visualize (θ_{vis}) the solution to the math problem.

The other vector in Equation (3.2) is $\mathbf{a}_i$, which contains the individual a_i (discrimination) parameters associated with each of the multiple dimensions in the model. The subscript i indicates that a is an *item* parameter. Suppose that Item 1 discriminates fairly well ($a_1 = 1.0$) between individuals who differ in terms of computation ability, but it is not so great ($a_2 = 0.8$) at discriminating with regard to visualization. Thus, $\mathbf{a}_1$ is the vector $\{1.0, 0.8\}$.

The third element in Equation (3.2) is the scalar c_i. You may recognize c_i as the intercept term from the slope-intercept notation introduced in the previous chapter. In the M2PL, c_i is still the intercept and is equal to $-\left(a_i'b_i\right)$, where b_i is a vector of item difficulty parameter estimates. Suppose it turns out that Item 1 is slightly easy ($b_1 = -0.2$) with regard to computation, but somewhat difficult ($b_2 = 0.5$) in terms of visualization; b_1 would then be the vector $\{-0.2, 0.5\}$. In person terms, a correct response is probable (that is, $P \geq 0.5$) if the test-taker is slightly below-average ability on the first dimension (computation) or well above-average ability on our second dimension (visualization). The intercept parameter c_i can then be obtained by plugging in the vectors $\mathbf{a}_i$ and $\mathbf{b}_i$:

$$c_i = -\left(\mathbf{a}_i'\mathbf{b}_i\right) = -\left(\begin{bmatrix} 1 \\ 0.8 \end{bmatrix}\begin{bmatrix} -0.2 & 0.5 \end{bmatrix}\right) = -0.2.$$

The vectors $\mathbf{a}_i$ and $\mathbf{b}_i$ can be used to obtain multidimensional discrimination and difficulty parameters of item i. However, interpretation of these parameters requires an in-depth discussion that we will leave for Chapter 5.

There is an obvious distinction between UIRT and MIRT models: In MIRT, the item response function is an m-dimensional surface rather than a 2-dimensional item response function. This surface can be visualized when $m = 2$. Figure 3.3 displays a hypothetical item response surface that would be produced by Equation (3.2) when $\mathbf{a}_i = \{1.0, 0.8\}$ and $c_i = -0.2$.

The x-axis and y-axis of both plots in Figure 3.3 represent the latent traits θ_1 and θ_2, and the z-axis in the figure on the left represents the probability of a correct response. The figure on the left illustrates a monotonically increasing surface: As θ_1 and θ_2 increase, the probability of responding correctly becomes higher. However, it is difficult to make out the exact degree

Figure 3.3 Item response surface (left) and contour plot (right) of an M2PL function with parameters $\mathbf{a}_i = \{1.0, 0.8\}$ and $c_i = -0.2$.

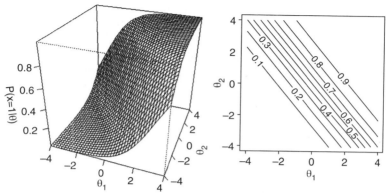

of probability that is associated with the various combinations of θ_1 and θ_2 in the surface plot. The plot on the right can help in this regard. Think of this contour plot as though you are looking down at the surface from directly overhead. The diagonal lines represent probabilities of 0.1 to 0.9 and their relationships with both latent traits. The leftmost diagonal indicates, for example, that a probability of 0.1 is expected when θ_1 is low, even if θ_2 is high. The rightmost diagonal shows that a probability of 0.9 is expected if, for example, person p demonstrates somewhat high ability on θ_1 and average ability on θ_2. Clearly, the item response surfaces and contour plots associated with a given MIRT model provide a wealth of information. We discuss various ways to dissect and interpret these figures in Chapter 5.

A straightforward empirical demonstration of the M2PL model is given by DeSimone and James (2015). These researchers conducted a psychometric analysis of the 22-item Conditional Reasoning Test of Aggression by considering 1-, 2-, and 3-parameter UIRT models, and they determined that although the (unidimensional) 2PL model was the best representation of the test data, it exhibited a nonignorable degree of multidimensionality in the form of local item dependence. Accordingly, the authors redefined aggression as a 2-dimensional construct (with externalizing and internalizing factors) rather than a unidimensional construct, and they were then able to successfully fit an M2PL model to the data. This strategy resulted in improved test-level and item-level goodness of fit. Further applications of the M2PL can be found throughout the literature on educational assessment (e.g., Ackerman, Gierl, & Walker, 2003; McKinley & Way, 1992) and psychological measurement (e.g., Colledani, Anselmi, & Robusto, 2019; Kolva, Rosenfeld, Liu, Pessin, & Breitbart, 2017; O'Connor, Comtois, Atkins, & Kerbrat, 2017), and empirical illustrations of the M2PL are often provided in more methodologically focused papers (e.g., Bolt & Lall, 2003).

Multidimensional 3-parameter logistic model. The M2PL discussed above can be extended to the multidimensional 3-parameter (M3PL) logistic model:

$$P\left(x_{ip} = 1 \mid \theta_p, \mathbf{a}_i, c_i, g_i\right) = g_i + \left(1 - g_i\right) \frac{\exp\left(\mathbf{a}_i \theta_p' + c_i\right)}{1 + \exp\left(\mathbf{a}_i \theta_p' + c_i\right)}. \tag{3.3}$$

Equation (3.3) looks just like the M2PL model presented in Equation (3.2), with the addition of g_i, the lower asymptote (or so-called guessing parameter) that reflects the nonzero probability of a correct response among examinees with extremely low abilities. If our example item is found to have a nonzero lower asymptote of, say, $g_i = 0.2$, this would imply that examinees who are especially low in computation *and* visualization will still have a .20 probability of providing a correct response. Figure 3.4 displays this scenario: At the low end of both latent traits, the response surface clearly never reaches zero.

Figure 3.4   Item response surface (left) and contour plot (right) of an M3PL function with parameters $\mathbf{a}_i = \{1.0, 0.8\}$, $c_i = -0.2$, and $g_i = 0.2$.

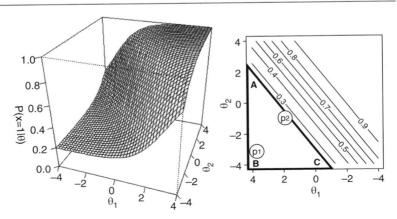

A closer look at Figure 3.4 reveals that it is not just the extreme low range of each latent trait that is associated with a nonzero probability of correct response. Using the 2-dimensional perspective of the contour plot, we can investigate the combinations of θ_1 and θ_2 that are associated with the same .20 "guessing" probability as the lowest ability levels. More specifically, all examinees whose combined abilities lie within the region ΔABC of the contour plot are similarly likely to respond correctly. To use Item 1 as an example, this means that person p_1, who has extremely low proficiency in computation and visualization ($\theta_{p_1} = \{-3, -4\}$) would be just as likely ($P = .20$) to give a correct response to the cheetah problem as person p_2, who has reasonably low proficiencies ($\theta_{p_2} = \{-2, -1\}$).

A useful illustration of the M3PL is presented by DeMars (2013) in the context of a Grade 4 science test of the Trends in International Mathematics and Science Study (TIMSS). In this tutorial, the author describes the statistical software that she used for estimating the M3PL; presents the discrimination, difficulty, and lower asymptotes parameter estimates of 11 multiple-choice science items; and discusses how to interpret the factor scores from a multidimensional model. Additional applications of the M3PL are given by McKinley and Way (1992) in the context of the Test of English as a Foreign Language and van Rijn, Sinharay, Haberman, and Johnson (2016) regarding the National Assessment of Educational Progress (NAEP).

Multidimensional 4-parameter logistic model. The M2PL model discussed above can also be extended to the multidimensional 4-parameter logistic (M4PL) model:

$$P\left(x_{ip} = 1 \mid \theta_p; \mathbf{a}_i, c_i, g_i, u_i\right) = g_i + \left(u_i - g_i\right)\frac{\exp\left(\mathbf{a}_i\theta_p' + c_i\right)}{1 + \exp\left(\mathbf{a}_i\theta_p' + c_i\right)} . \quad (3.4)$$

The M4PL model in Equation (3.4) expands the M3PL model in Equation (3.3) by adding u_i, an upper asymptote parameter that represents a non-1.0 probability of correct response among examinees with extremely high abilities on all of the θ dimensions. If our example item was found to have a significantly non-1.0 u_i parameter, this would indicate that even examinees with exceptionally high proficiencies in both computation *and* visualization would not be expected to have a 1.0 probability of providing a correct response. A visual representation of the M4PL is given in Figure 3.5. Here, the upper asymptote equals .8, meaning that individuals of the highest math and reading abilities only have a .8 probability of answering this item correctly. All examinees located within the region ΔDEF of the

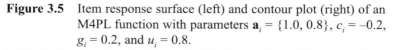

Figure 3.5   Item response surface (left) and contour plot (right) of an M4PL function with parameters $\mathbf{a}_i = \{1.0, 0.8\}$, $c_i = -0.2$, $g_i = 0.2$, and $u_i = 0.8$.

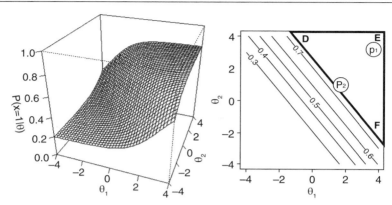

contour plot have equally likely probabilities of correct response. In terms of our example item, person p_1, who is extraordinarily high in both computation and visualization ($\theta_{p_1} = \{4, 3\}$), has the same correct response probability ($P = 0.8$) as person p_2, whose proficiencies are moderately high ($\theta_{p_2} = \{2, 1\}$). Possible explanations for such a result are given in the previous chapter's discussion of the unidimensional 4PL model. Note also that the M4PL estimates the lower asymptote as well as the upper, though by constraining g_i to 0 in Equation (3.4), the model becomes an inverted M3PL in which the lower asymptote is fixed at 0 and the upper asymptote may deviate from 1.0. Further constraints can be applied to the M4PL to produce the M3PL (when $u_i = 1$) and M2PL (when $u_i = 1$ and $g_i = 0$).

To the best of this author's knowledge, there are currently no published applications of the M4PL model. However, Culpepper (2017) developed a multidimensional 4-parameter normal ogive model that is closely related (and conceptually identical) to the M4PL model. He successfully applied this model to data from the eighth-grade math and reading tests of the NAEP. His findings revealed that the upper asymptote parameter was estimated below .95 in nearly half of the items on both the math and reading tests. The author points out that failure to account for this "slipping" effect may adversely affect test information and measurement precision. While further M4PL applications have not yet been published, recent advances in estimation strategies (discussed in Chapter 7) and computing power have increased the feasibility of fitting this complex model to multidimensional test data.

Multidimensional Rasch model. The simplest compensatory MIRT model is the multidimensional Rasch model (MRM; Adams, Wilson, & Wang, 1997). For dichotomous data, the MRM is given by

$$P\left(x_{ip} = 1 \mid \mathbf{\theta}_p; \mathbf{a}_i, c_i, \right) = \frac{\exp\left(a_i\mathbf{\theta}'_p + c_i\right)}{1 + \exp\left(a_i\mathbf{\theta}'_p + c_i\right)}. \tag{3.5}$$

This equation should look familiar—it is identical to the M2PL equation presented earlier. The difference is that in the MRM, $\mathbf{a}_i$ is a user-specified vector indicating which latent dimensions a are associated with the given item i. Note that $\mathbf{a}_i$ is not statistically estimated by the model; instead, the user inputs values to denote which dimension(s) each item is measuring. Between-item dimensionality is represented by a vector such as $\mathbf{a}_i = \{1, 0\}$, which would indicate that of the two dimensions in the model, item i is targeting measurement of the first dimension and not the second. Within-item dimensionality would be represented by a vector such as $\mathbf{a}_1 = \{1, 0.5\}$, which would indicate that a correct response to Item 1 (our example item) involves both dimensions, though the first dimension is deemed to be twice as important as the second dimension. Of course, such specifications would require content expertise and would ideally be based on strong theory regarding the item under consideration.

An interesting illustration of the MRM is provided by Pretz et al. (2016) in the context of traumatic brain injury. In this study, the MRM was used to investigate the difficulty of each item on the Functional Independence Measure, which includes three subscales measuring cognitive functioning, self-care, and mobility. Rather than fitting a separate unidimensional Rasch model to each of these subscales, the authors simultaneously estimated the item parameters of each subscale. By accounting for the relationships among the subscales, the multidimensional approach improved the statistical accuracy of the results and led to a deeper understanding of the functional independence of persons with neurotrauma. Additional MRM applications are given by Sam, Li, and Lo (2016) in the measurement of attitudes toward people with intellectual disabilities, and Hartig and Harsch (2017) in estimating the reading and listening comprehension of English-language learners.

R Code

Conveniently, the mirt package uses similar code for UIRT and MIRT modeling. In the multidimensional case, the `model` argument of the `mirt()` command will reflect either the number of latent traits you wish to estimate (in an exploratory factor analysis sense) or a particular item factor structure (in a confirmatory factor analysis sense). For example, if you want to explore a 2-factor MIRT model, your code would be

```
output <- mirt(data = mydata, model = 2).
```

You can then add the `itemtype` argument as before, though the presence of more than one dimension in the `model` argument will cause the `mirt()` command to automatically estimate a multidimensional model. That is, `itemtype` = `'2PL'`, `'3PL'`, or `'4PL'` will yield the M2PL, M3PL, or M4PL, respectively.

Partially Compensatory MIRT Models

We turn now to the partially compensatory class of MIRT models. The 4-parameter extension of Sympson's (1978) partially compensatory model is given by

$$P\left(x_{ip}=1\mid \theta_p; \mathbf{a}_i, \mathbf{b}_i, g_i, u_i\right) = g_i + \left(u_i - g_i\right)\prod_{m=1}^{M}\frac{\exp\left[a_{im}\left(\theta_{pm}-b_{im}\right)\right]}{1+\exp\left[a_{im}\left(\theta_{pm}-b_{im}\right)\right]}. \quad (3.6)$$

Here, the vector $\mathbf{b}_i$ contains the difficulty parameters associated with item i. The intercept parameter c_i that we saw in earlier models does not appear in Equation (3.6) because partially compensatory models require a discrimination parameter and a difficulty parameter for each latent trait. The subscript m denotes a specific latent trait (of the M possible latent traits in the model). Thus, the partially compensatory model takes the dimension-specific probabilities (as a function of person and item parameters) and multiplies them together to obtain the overall probability of a correct response. Note that just as in the 4PL compensatory model, the earlier partially compensatory model can be reduced to simpler models by constraining certain parameters (e.g., a partially compensatory 2-parameter model can be specified by fixing the upper asymptote $[u_i]$ to 1.0 and the lower asymptote $[g_i]$ to 0.0).

Taking a closer look at Equation (3.6), we see that this model is partially compensatory because of its multiplicative nature. If the respondent exhibits low proficiency on any one of the latent traits involved in producing a correct response, then his or her overall probability of a correct response will be low. Recall that our partially compensatory interpretation of Item 1 relates to reading and math abilities. Let us suppose that example Item 1 has a discrimination parameter of $a_1 = 1.0$ and a difficulty of $b_1 = 0.5$ with regard to reading proficiency. If Allan (denoted as person A) is a poor reader (e.g., $\theta_{A.read} = -2.0$), then the probability P_{read} associated with the latent dimension representing reading ability will be very low, as determined by supplying these values to Equation (3.6):

$$P_{read}\left(x=1\,|\,\theta_{A.read} = -2.0,\ a_{1.read} = 1.0,\ b_{1.read} = 0.5\right) = .076.$$

That is, Allan's reading proficiency will result in an especially low probability, which will be multiplied by the probability P_{math} associated with his latent math trait to produce the overall probability of a correct response. Suppose for the sake of convenience that the math component of Item 1 is just as discriminatory and difficult as the reading component but that Allan is a math whiz such that $\theta_{A.math} = 3$. Plugging these values into Equation (3.6) gives

$$P_{math}\left(x=1\,|\,\theta_{A.math} = 3.0,\ a_{1.math} = 1.0,\ b_{1.math} = 0.5\right) = .924.$$

Although Allan clearly has impressive math ability, the overall probability is found by multiplying the individual reading and math probabilities, which in this case is just $.924 \times .076 = .070$. In other words, excelling at math will not compensate for insufficient reading ability; both skills are necessary in order to correctly respond to Item 1. Interested readers could compute the probabilities associated with high reading and low math abilities and would arrive at the same conclusion.

The partially compensatory model in Equation (3.6) can be visualized when there are two latent dimensions involved in responding correctly. Figure 3.6 displays examples of the response surface and contour plot produced by a partially compensatory M2PL (or PC-M2PL) MIRT model with parameter vectors $\mathbf{a}_i = \{1.0, 0.8\}$ and $\mathbf{b}_i = \{-0.2, 0.5\}$ (i.e., the same parameter values that we saw in the compensatory M2PL example). In partially compensatory modeling, the item response surface resembles a hill that only peaks when both θ_1 *and* θ_2 are high.

The contour plot is much more revealing than the surface plot. The leftmost curve shows, for example, that respondents who are low on the first latent trait (e.g., $\theta_1 < -2$) only have a $P = 0.1$ probability of responding correctly even if their location along the second latent trait is extremely high (e.g., $\theta_2 > 3$; and vice versa). Furthermore, the $P = 0.5$ contour line indicates that a .5 or greater probability of responding correctly requires above-average proficiency with regard to both traits (e.g., θ_1 *and* θ_2 must both be greater than zero).

40

Figure 3.6 Item response surface (left) and contour plot (right) of a PC-M2PL function with parameters $\mathbf{a}_i = \{1.0, 0.8\}$ and $\mathbf{b}_i = \{-0.2, 0.5\}$.

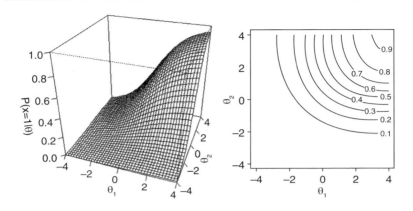

There are two key differences between the compensatory and PC contour plots. In the compensatory examples from earlier, we saw contours that were linear and parallel, but here, the contours are curved and not necessarily parallel. More specifically, consecutive PC contour curves may be close to one another at certain combinations of θ but farther apart at others, depending on the discrimination parameters in $\mathbf{a}_i$. In Figure 3.6, it is difficult to discern this lack of parallelism because the discrimination parameters are close in magnitude ($\mathbf{a}_i = \{1.0, 0.8\}$). In contrast, consider the example in Figure 3.7, in which the difference between the discrimination parameters is much greater ($\mathbf{a}_i = \{0.5, 2.0\}$).

Suppose these plots reflect the parameters associated with our cheetah word problem, where θ_1 is reading ability and θ_2 is math ability. As math ability increases (i.e., starting at the nearest region of the surface plot and moving away), the probability of a correct response increases fairly rapidly around $\theta_2 = 0$, especially when reading ability is above average, and then begins to plateau once $\theta_2 = 1$. In this example, the contour lines are clearly not parallel. The first latent dimension is much less discriminating than the second, so the vertical portions of each curve (reflecting different locations along the θ_1 continuum) are quite far apart while the horizontal portions (reflecting different locations along the θ_2 continuum) are close together. This differential spacing illustrates the much greater role played by θ_2. In Chapter 5, we discuss additional ways to interpret the results obtained from fitting a PC MIRT model to item response data.

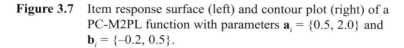

Figure 3.7 Item response surface (left) and contour plot (right) of a PC-M2PL function with parameters $\mathbf{a}_i = \{0.5, 2.0\}$ and $\mathbf{b}_i = \{-0.2, 0.5\}$.

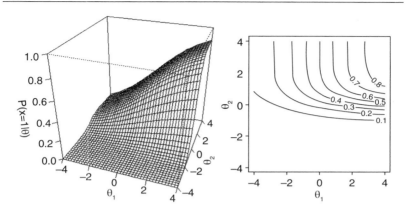

PC MIRT models are employed far less often than their compensatory counterparts, and empirical applications are scarce. However, in a pair of simulation studies, Buchholz and Hartig (2018) demonstrate the usefulness of the PC M2PL in the context of word problems that require both mathematical ability and reading proficiency. Furthermore, these authors underscore the potential for statistical bias that can arise if practitioners assume that the relationship between test dimensions is compensatory. Further PC MIRT modeling examples are provided in methodological papers by Bolt and Lall (2003) regarding an English placement exam and Rizopoulos and Moustaki (2008) in modeling responses to the Workplace Industrial Relations Survey.

R Code

The mirt package accommodates partially compensatory 2PL and 3PL MIRT models via `itemtype = 'PC2PL' or 'PC3PL'`.

Additional MIRT Models for Dichotomous Data

The analysis of multidimensional item response data is not limited to the dichotomous and polytomous models discussed earlier. This section briefly presents two advanced multidimensional models that have emerged in recent years. While there are additional variants of MIRT models that could be discussed, these were selected because they expand upon two key notions discussed earlier: compensation and continuity.

Variable compensation models. Although the previous discussion presented the relationship between latent traits as either compensatory or partially compensatory, it is actually possible to measure the degree of compensation. Variable compensation models (Ackerman & Turner, 2003; Bolt & Lall, 2003; Spray, Ackerman, & Carlson, 1986) allow the strength of the compensatory relationship between dimensions to be empirically estimated. For example, Spray et al. (1986) introduced the generalized multidimensional IRT (GMIRT) model, shown here in a 2-dimensional formulation:

$$P\left(R_{ip} = 1 \mid \boldsymbol{\theta}_p, \mathbf{a}_i, b_i, \mu_c\right) = \frac{\exp\left(f_1 + f_2\right)}{1 + \exp\left(f_1 + f_2\right) + \mu_c\left[\exp\left(f_1\right) + \exp\left(f_2\right)\right]}, \quad (3.7)$$

where $f_1 = a_{1i}\left(\theta_{1p} - b_{1i}\right)$ and $f_2 = a_{2i}\left(\theta_{2p} - b_{2i}\right)$. The parameter μ_c is a continuous item-level indicator parameter that ranges from 0 (a purely compensatory model) to 1 (a purely noncompensatory model). By freely estimating μ_c, the GMIRT model allows the data to determine whether the relationship between traits is more or less compensatory. That is, rather than deciding a priori whether the interaction between latent traits is compensatory or not, a researcher can apply the GMIRT model and empirically estimate the degree (or lack) of compensation.

Diagnostic classification models. An alternate approach to measurement is offered by a class of models known as diagnostic classification models (DCMs; Rupp, Templin, & Henson, 2010). The MIRT models discussed above facilitate the measurement of multiple *continuous* traits. DCMs are similar to MIRT models, except that the focus is on measuring multiple *categorical* (usually dichotomous) attributes. In educational applications, these attributes typically represent the particular skills underlying a correct response probability. Thus, DCMs are an increasingly popular class of models that expands upon basic IRT analysis by providing for each examinee a description of the mastery/nonmastery of the various attributes that make up each item. For example, a correct response to the math item $\frac{5}{3} - \frac{3}{4}$ requires mastery of three attributes: finding a common denominator, column borrowing to subtract the second numerator from the first, and subtracting numerators (de la Torre & Douglas, 2004).

Details regarding the formulation and use of DCMs are provided later, but as an introduction, consider the following insight into student performance that can be obtained by fitting a DCM. For each test-taker, a DCM will provide the probability that he or she has mastered each of the requisite attributes (coded such that 0 denotes nonmastery and 1 denotes mastery). On a math test, for example, a DCM might indicate that Student A has mastered finding a common denominator, column borrowing, and subtracting numerators; her mastery pattern would be {111}. Student B may have mastered only the first skill, so his mastery pattern would be {100}. These patterns of mastery, or "attribute profiles," can be quite beneficial to teaching and learning activities; by identifying areas of nonmastery, the teacher can offer supplementary instruction or educational interventions that target specific academic shortcomings. Returning to the example, the DCM results could prompt the teacher to give Student B additional training in column borrowing and subtracting numerators so that he might master these particular skills.

While numerous DCMs exist, simplicity of estimation and interpretation makes the deterministic input, noisy "and" gate (DINA) model perhaps the most popular choice for diagnostic cognitive test data (de la Torre & Douglas, 2004; Haertel, 1989; Huebner & Wang, 2011; Junker & Sijtsma, 2001; Tatsuoka, 1983). The DINA model is partially compensatory, or conjunctive, meaning that presence/mastery of one attribute will not fully compensate for absence/nonmastery of other attributes. The "and gate" portion of the DINA acronym indicates that all item attributes must be present/mastered in order to endorse an item or produce the correct response. The DINA model is formulated as

$$P\left(y_i = 1 \mid \alpha_c\right) = g_i^{1-\xi_{ic}} \left(1 - s_i\right)^{\xi_{ic}}. \tag{3.8}$$

The left side of Equation (3.8) represents the probability of a correct response ($y_i = 1$) to item i, given an attribute pattern α_c of latent class c, where $\alpha_c = \{m_1, m_2, \ldots, M\}$ for the M attributes that must be mastered in order to provide a correct response. For example, if a correct response requires mastery of two attributes m_1 and m_2 and 0/1 indicate nonmastery/ mastery of the given skill m, then there are four possible attribute classes: $\alpha_c = \{00\}, \{01\}, \{10\},$ or $\{11\}$. Thus, an individual of the first class $\alpha_c = \{00\}$ has mastered neither m_1 nor m_2, while an individual of the second class $\alpha_c = \{01\}$ has mastered m_2 but not m_1, and so on.

The right side of Equation (3.8) shows that the probability of providing a correct response in the DINA model is contingent on two parameters: g_i and s_i. The guessing parameter g_i reflects the probability of providing a correct answer even though the student has not mastered all of the attributes necessary for correctly answering item i. The slipping parameter s_i, on the other hand, represents the probability of providing an incorrect answer even if the student has mastered all attributes related to item i.

A key component of any DCM is the Q-matrix, an item-by-attribute matrix that is used to identify, for each item, the attributes that must be mastered in order to register a correct response. If mastery of a certain attribute m is required to correctly answer item i, then Q-matrix entry $q_{im} = 1$; if attribute m is not associated with item i, then $q_{im} = 0$. The DINA model is thus characterized by a logic gate given by

$$\xi_{ic} = \prod_{m=1}^{M} \alpha_{cm}^{q_{im}},$$

which indicates whether the respondent has mastered *all M* of the attributes α_{cm} required for a correct response to item i, according to the Q-matrix q. In the DINA model, ξ_{ic} is a latent variable that takes on the value of 1 if student j has mastered (i.e., $q_{im} = 1$) all of the attributes α_{cm} required by item i, and 0 otherwise. In other words, if any attribute α_{cm} is equal to zero, then ξ_{ic} is also equal to zero. By plugging in $\xi_{ic} = 0$ (i.e., at least one of the required attributes has not been mastered), we see the function of the gate:

$$P\left(y_i = 1 \mid \alpha_c\right) = g_i^1 \left(1 - s_i\right)^0 = g_i.$$

That is, if the respondent has not mastered all required attributes, then the probability of a correct response is equivalent to guessing.

Overall, DCMs offer a more fine-grained analysis than that allowed by MIRT models. Both of these model classes can be used to better understand the relationships among multiple latent variables, but they have different goals. If the goal is to estimate the respondent's location along more than one latent trait (be it ability, proficiency, or severity), then MIRT modeling would be the appropriate choice. If the goal is to estimate the respondent's mastery profile with regard to more than one attribute, then diagnostic classification modeling would be useful. The earlier discussion is just a brief introduction to DCMs; interested readers can consult Rupp et al. (2010) for a thorough treatment of this topic.

Informative applications of DCMs are offered by Jurich and Bradshaw (2013) in an analysis of higher education student learning outcomes, and Ravand (2016) regarding a high-stakes reading comprehension test. Both of these papers present accessible illustrations of DCMs in the real world and highlight the advantages of the DCM approach over standard IRT modeling. Further examples are given in various research contexts, including reading assessment (Chen & de la Torre, 2014; Ravand, Barati, & Widhiarso, 2013), mathematics testing (Bradshaw, Izsák, Templin, & Jacobson, 2014; Y. Lee, Park, & Taylan, 2011), and psychiatric diagnosis (de la Torre, van der Ark, & Rossi, 2015).

R Code

For diagnostic classification modeling in R, see the GDINA (Ma & de la Torre, 2019) or CDM (Robitzsch, Kiefer, George, & Uenlue, 2017) packages.

Recent Advances in Dichotomous MIRT Modeling

Additional MIRT models for dichotomous data are available, though they are beyond the scope of the present book. Examples include the MIRT unfolding (aka "ideal point" or "proximity") model, in which a binary agree/disagree-type item is endorsed if it aligns with the respondent's opinion (Maydeu-Olivares, Hernández, & McDonald, 2006); the item factor copula model for handling local independence violations (Braeken, 2011); and the multidimensional latent class model that includes a discrete latent trait distribution (Bartolucci, 2007), among others.

Chapter 4

MIRT MODELS FOR POLYTOMOUS DATA

MIRT models are also capable of accommodating items that are measured on a polytomous scale. Consider another example, in which Fumiko, a ninth-grade student, is presented with a psychological test item:

Item 2: I enjoy social situations.

  ○ Always   ○ Sometimes   ○ Never

The item is polytomous because Fumiko is presented with multiple response options. Suppose that a clinical psychologist has hypothesized that a response of *Never* to Item 2 reflects a relatively high degree of anxiety (θ_{anx}) and/or introversion (θ_{int}). The probability of Fumiko's response to this 2-dimensional polytomous item could be modeled using a number of (compensatory[1]) polytomous MIRT models. We discuss three such models in this chapter.

The multidimensional graded response model. Recall from Chapter 2 that the GRM is a difference model: The boundaries between adjacent response categories are modeled as a series of ordered dichotomies. Specifically,

$$P(k) = P^*(k) - P^*(k+1),$$

meaning the probability of selecting a particular polytomous response option k can be found by examining the difference between the probability of selecting k or higher versus $k+1$ or higher. Recall that $P^*(k=0) = 1$, because the probability of responding in category 0 or higher is a sure thing. Similarly, if K is the number of categories, then $P^*(k = K + 1) = 0$, because there is no category higher than K.

In Example Item 2, this means there will be three dichotomies, where $0 = Always$, $1 = Sometimes$, and $2 = Never$:

1. $P(k = 0) = P^*(k = 0, 1, \text{ or } 2) - P^*(k = 1, \text{ or } 2) = 1 - P^*(k = 1, \text{ or } 2)$
2. $P(k = 1) = P^*(k = 1, \text{ or } 2) - P^*(k = 2)$
3. $P(k = 2) = P^*(k = 2) - P^*(m + 1) = P^*(k = 2) - 0 = P^*(k = 2)$

---

[1] To this author's knowledge, partially compensatory polytomous MIRT models are yet to be developed.

Essentially, the GRM fits each of these dichotomies with a 2PL, thereby estimating the examinee's most likely response choice, given his or her location along the latent trait continuum. A standard GRM analysis will indicate, for example, that an individual with social anxiety disorder will be most likely to select *Never* regarding enjoyment of social situations.

The multidimensional graded response model (MGRM) follows the same logic as the original GRM but yields response category surfaces that reflect the probability of selecting a particular response option, conditional on multiple latent traits. The logistic representation of the MGRM (de Ayala, 1994) is given by

$$P\left(x_{ip} = k \mid \boldsymbol{\theta}_p; \mathbf{a}_i, \boldsymbol{\tau}_i\right) = \frac{\exp\left[\sum_m a_m (\theta_m - \tau_k)\right]}{1 + \exp\left[\sum_m a_m (\theta_m - \tau_k)\right]}, \qquad (4.1)$$

where $\mathbf{a}_i$ is a vector of discrimination parameters for item i on each latent trait m, and $\boldsymbol{\tau}_i$ contains the threshold parameters for each category k within item i.

The separate response functions for each category are perhaps best understood by substituting some precise values. Suppose that Fumiko is fairly low in anxiety ($\theta_{anx} = -0.5$) and high in introversion ($\theta_{int} = 1$), such that $\boldsymbol{\theta}_p = \{-0.5, 1\}$. Suppose also that our example item has discrimination parameters of $\mathbf{a}_i = \{1, 1.5\}$ and thresholds of $\boldsymbol{\tau}_i = \{-.25, .75\}$. The probability of selecting *Always* (i.e., $k = 0$) is found by $P(k = 0) = 1 - P^*(k - 1 \text{ or } 2)$, as presented earlier. The latter term represents the boundary between category 0 (*Always*) and category 1 (*Sometimes*) or higher, which is

$$P^*(k = 1 \text{ or } 2) = \frac{\exp\left[1\left(-0.5 - (-.25)\right) + 1.5\left(1 - (-.25)\right)\right]}{1 + \exp\left[1\left(-0.5 - (-.25)\right) + 1.5\left(1 - (-.25)\right)\right]} = .83.$$

Thus, $P(k = 0) = 1 - P^*(k = 1 \text{ or } 2) = 1 - .83 - .17$. That is, there is a low probability ($P = .17$) that Fumiko will select *Always* with regard to the item about enjoying social situations. This makes sense—Fumiko has fairly high levels of introversion, so socializing may not be an activity that she wants to engage in too often.

The probability that Fumiko will choose *Sometimes* (i.e., $k = 1$) as her response is found by taking the difference between the first and second boundaries; that is, $P(k = 1) = P^*(k = 1 \text{ or } 2) = P^*(k = 2)$. The first boundary is presented earlier, and the second boundary, between category $k = 1$ (*Sometimes*) and category $k = 2$ (*Never*), is given by

$$P^*\left(k=2\right)=\frac{\exp\left[1\left(-0.5-.75\right)+1.5\left(1-.75\right)\right]}{1+\exp\left[1\left(-0.5-.75\right)+1.5\left(1-.75\right)\right]}=.29.$$

Taking the difference results in $P(k=1) = .83 - .29 = 54$. There is a moderately high probability ($P = .54$) that Fumiko will respond that she *Sometimes* enjoys social situations.

Finally, the probability that Fumiko will select *Never* (i.e., $k = 2$) is found by $P(k = 2) = P^*(k = 2)$. We already computed this value in the previous equation. Thus, there is a moderately low (.29) probability that Fumiko will respond that she *Never* enjoys social situations. Taking all three response category surfaces into consideration, we conclude that given Fumiko's underlying levels of anxiety and introversion, she is most likely to respond that she *Sometimes* enjoys social situations.

The MGRM category response surfaces of Example Item 2 are shown in Figure 4.1. We can see that each response option k is associated with a separate response surface. These surfaces represent the most likely response choice at each combination of θ_1 and θ_2.

Figure 4.1　Category response surfaces of a MGRM response function with parameters $\mathbf{a}_i = \{1, 1.5\}$ and $\mathbf{\tau}_i = \{-.25, .75\}$.

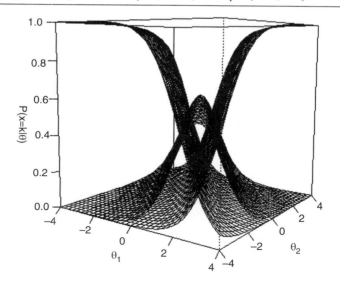

50

As you may expect, these intricate polytomous response surface plots can be better visualized using contour plots. Figure 4.2 displays the separate surfaces for each of the k response options to Item 2 alongside the linear contour plots. The line width of each contour has been modified to reflect the magnitude of the response option probability, such that wider

Figure 4.2 Separate category response surfaces of a MGRM function with parameters $\mathbf{a}_i = \{1, 1.5\}$ and $\boldsymbol{\tau}_i = \{-.25, .75\}$.

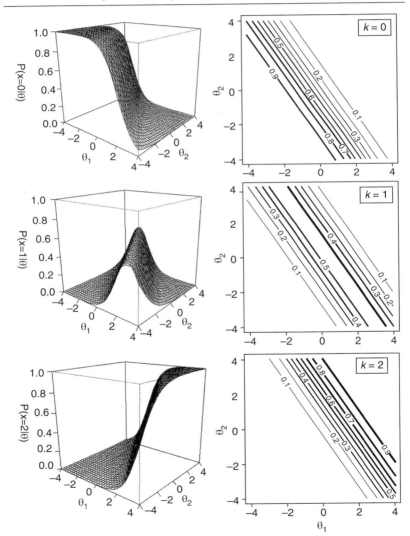

lines represent higher probabilities. The top panel shows that option $k = 0$ (*Always*) is highly probable when both θ_1 (anxiety) and θ_2 (introversion) are low. For example, this top panel tells us that it would be fairly unlikely ($P \approx .3$) for a respondent with average levels of anxiety and introversion ($\theta_1 = \theta_2 = 0$) to select option *Always*. The middle panel of Figure 4.2 displays the contour representation of the $k = 1$ (*Sometimes*) category response surface. Here, the thickness of the lines reflects the hill-shaped surface of the middle category, which peaks along a diagonal region of the θ-plane. This response option is the likely choice of individuals with average levels of anxiety and introversion, as well as those with extremely low anxiety and extremely high introversion (and vice versa). Finally, the bottom panel of Figure 4.2 displays the contours related to the *Never* response option, which is the most likely choice for persons with high anxiety and high introversion.

Polytomous MIRT models are applied less frequently than the simpler dichotomous models, though a handful of successful real-world applications demonstrate their utility. A clear illustration of the MGRM is presented by Kilgus, Bonifay, von der Embse, Allen, and Eklund (2018) in their analysis of the 5-point Likert-type data from the Social, Academic, and Emotional Behavior Risk Screener. The authors employed the MGRM to estimate the item parameters and to ascertain the person locations (i.e., IRT-scaled scores) along the social, academic, and emotional behavior dimensions. Another helpful example is given by Toland, Sulis, Giambona, Porcu, and Campbell (2017), who used the MGRM to measure respondents' behavioral intentions towards people with autism.

The multidimensional (generalized) partial credit model. The multidimensional extension of the generalized partial credit model (MGPCM; Yao & Schwarz, 2006) is given by

$$P\left(x_{ip} = k \mid \boldsymbol{\theta}_p; \mathbf{a}_i, \boldsymbol{\tau}_{ix}\right) = \frac{\exp\left(ka_i\boldsymbol{\theta}'_p - \sum_{x=0}^{k} \tau_{ix}\right)}{\sum_{m=0}^{K_i} \exp\left(ma_i\boldsymbol{\theta}'_p - \sum_{x=0}^{m} \tau_{ix}\right)}, \qquad (4.2)$$

where k represents the person's selected response category for item i, m represents all $K_i + 1$ possible categories for item i, and τ_{ix} is the threshold parameter for item i and response x (with the constraint that $\tau_{i0} = 0$). Recall from Chapter 2 that the GPCM is a divide-by-total model. We see the same formulation in the MGPCM: The numerator is related to the person's response, and the denominator reflects the sum of all response probabilities. The category response surfaces of a hypothetical 2-dimensional MGPCM would look quite similar to the MGRM presented in Figures 4.1 and 4.2 and are therefore not shown here.

It is important to note a key difference in interpretation between the unidimensional and multidimensional forms of the GPCM. In the unidimensional model (based on Equation [2.5]), we see separate item difficulty and threshold parameters, but in Equation (4.2), this is not the case. Furthermore, the threshold parameters are interpreted differently in the MGPCM due to the fact that $\boldsymbol{\theta}_p$ is a vector (containing estimates of θ for each of the latent traits underlying response choice), but the τ_{ix} values are scalars (reflecting the boundaries between categories for item i). To rectify this problem, the exponents in the numerator of Equation (4.2) are set to equality for adjacent response categories (e.g., $k = Always$ and $k + 1 = Sometimes$ in our example item):

$$k\mathbf{a}_i\boldsymbol{\theta}'_p - \sum_{x=0}^{k}\tau_{ix} = \left(k+1\right)\mathbf{a}_i\boldsymbol{\theta}'_p - \sum_{x=0}^{k+1}\tau_{ix}.$$

Solving this equality results in

$$0 = \mathbf{a}_i\boldsymbol{\theta}'_p - \tau_{i,k+1},$$

which represents the combinations of $\boldsymbol{\theta}$ at which the category response surfaces for k and $k + 1$ intersect (for $k = [0, \ldots , K - 1]$), as depicted by the diagonal lines in Figure 4.3.

The diagonal lines in this figure indicate the combinations of θ_1 and θ_2 that are associated with the thresholds (or "steps") between response options. In the context of our psychological test item, a respondent with average anxiety ($\theta_1 = 0$) and low introversion ($\theta_2 = -2$) is expected to select *Always* ($k = 0$). If this respondent increases in anxiety and/or extraversion, then he or she will cross the threshold between $k = 0$ and $k = 1$, making *Sometimes* ($k = 1$) the more likely response choice.

An instructive application of the MGPCM appears in an analysis of a vocational interest inventory by Wetzel and Hell (2014). These authors contrasted the MGPCM with its unidimensional counterpart and showed how accounting for multidimensionality not only improves the statistical accuracy of the results but may also lead to more interesting substantive interpretations. Another MGPCM application is offered by C. Chen, Xie, Clifford, Chen, and Squires (2018) in their analysis of polytomous data from a developmental screening questionnaire.

The multidimensional nominal response model. Although our polytomous example item clearly has ordered categories, it would be possible to fit the responses to this item with a multidimensional nominal response model. Thissen, Cai, and Bock (2010) reparameterized the nominal

Figure 4.3 Thresholds between category response surfaces in a MGPCM function with parameters $\mathbf{a}_i = \{1, 1\}$, $\boldsymbol{\tau}_1 = \{-1, 1\}$, and $\boldsymbol{\tau}_2 = \{-1, 1\}$.

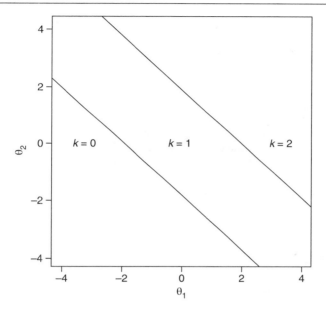

response model in order to give it a single overall discrimination parameter and a scoring function (i.e., a set of contrasts among the *a* parameters; see Muraki, 1992). An additional reason for this reparameterization was to accommodate multiple latent traits. The resulting multidimensional nominal response model (MNRM) is given by

$$P\left(x_{ip} = k \mid \boldsymbol{\theta}; \mathbf{a}^*, \mathbf{a}^s, \mathbf{c}\right) = \frac{\exp\left(a'^* a_k^s \boldsymbol{\theta} + c_k\right)}{\sum_i \left(\exp\left(a'^* a_i^s \boldsymbol{\theta} + c_i\right)\right)}. \tag{4.3}$$

In this formulation, $\mathbf{a}^*$ is the overall (multiplicative) discrimination parameter, which indicates the direction of steepest slope (an issue we explore in more detail in the next chapter). $\mathbf{a}^s$ represents the scoring functions, which are assumed to be the same in all directions. This model can be used with survey response data in which the data are truly nominal, multiple-choice data in which there is one correct answer and a set of unordered distractor options, as well as ordinal (e.g., Likert-type) data. In this last case, the MNRM can be used to confirm that the hypothesized ordering of response options aligns with how people actually respond (i.e., is *Sometimes* actually located somewhere between *Always* and *Never* as hypothesized?) (Preston, Reise, Cai, & Hays, 2011). Thissen et al. (2010) note that when the model is parameterized so that the scoring functions are linear (e.g., $a^s = 0, 1, 2, \ldots, m-1$), then the model is equivalent to the MGPCM presented in Equation (4.2). Recent extensions and refinements to the MNRM have been made by Revuelta (2014). In the context of our example item, the MNRM would be expected to produce similar category response surfaces and contour plots, so they are not shown here.

The MNRM is a relatively complex model and has not been applied as often as the other polytomous MIRT models. However, in his methodological paper on the MNRM, Revuelta (2014) presents an empirical example using responses from an undergraduate data analysis exam. The author illustrates how to estimate and interpret the MNRM parameters and discusses important challenges associated with applying this advanced model. Interested readers may also consult Bolt and Johnson (2009), who present a particularly inventive application of the MNRM with regard to a self-report tobacco dependence survey. Rather than simply estimating the parameters of the nominal items, these researchers used the MNRM to model individual response styles and identify differential item functioning.

R Code

In the mirt package, itemtype = 'graded', 'gpcm', or 'nominal' will estimate the MGRM, MGPCM, or MNRM, respectively, whenever the model argument indicates multidimensionality.

Additional Polytomous MIRT Models

In addition to the models described earlier, there are additional MIRT models for polytomous data. Interested readers may want to explore models such as the multidimensional Rasch partial credit model (Kelderman, 1996), the multidimensional Rasch model for repeated item administrations (Andersen, 1985), the multidimensional Rasch model for learning and change (Embretson, 1991), or the multidimensional random coefficients multinomial logit model (Briggs & Wilson, 2003). While these models examine polytomous data in complex and interesting ways, they are beyond the scope of this volume.

Chapter 5

DESCRIPTIVE MIRT STATISTICS

There are a number of interesting and informative ways to describe the results of a MIRT analysis. This chapter presents several descriptive MIRT statistics, including multidimensional difficulty and discrimination parameters, conditional probabilities, information functions, and predicted item scores, among other descriptives. We focus mostly on the compensatory M2PL model, though most of the descriptive statistics and interpretations that we explore can be directly extended to the more complex dichotomous and polytomous MIRT models presented in the previous chapters. We begin our discussion by detailing three descriptive statistics that are essential to comprehending MIRT modeling: the θ-space, the multidimensional discrimination index, and the multidimensional difficulty index.

The θ-Space

The θ scale in UIRT, while technically unbounded, is often considered within a reasonable range, such as -3 to $+3$, as shown at the top of Figure 5.1. Although the following terms are not typically used in UIRT, we can think of the UIRT continuum as the *axis of measurement* and the zero point as the *origin* of this axis. Item difficulty and respondent ability parameters are then located at various points along this axis, where the origin represents average difficulty/ability, negative values indicate below-average difficulty/ability, and positive values indicate above-average difficulty/ability.

MIRT introduces a deceptively complex problem: When more than one latent trait is related to the probability of a correct response, then the scale is no longer a line. In the 2-dimensional case, there are two axes—one for each dimension—which results in a latent trait *plane* rather than a line. This plane can be displayed using a Cartesian coordinate system as in Figure 5.1 (bottom). The axes reflect the two latent traits, θ_1 and θ_2, that are associated with the given item. In this example, each dimension ranges from -3 to $+3$, and the origin $(0, 0)$ is indicated by the black dot in the center. When we discuss, for example, the multidimensional difficulty parameter of the M2PL model, the difficulty estimate must be interpreted relative to the origin of this plane. This introduces an important aspect of MIRT: While UIRT parameters are located to the left or right of the zero point, MIRT

56

Figure 5.1 Unidimensional θ scale (top) and multidimensional **θ** plane (bottom).

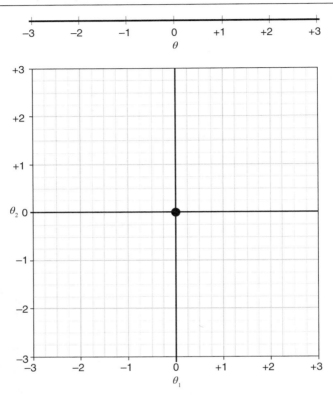

parameters can be located *in any direction* from the (0, 0) point. So a MIRT difficulty parameter of 1.5 in the direction of 30 degrees from the origin has a different meaning than a MIRT difficulty parameter of 1.5 in the direction of, say, −50 degrees from the origin.

Regarding the discussion that follows, we should keep two issues in mind. First, when there are more than two latent traits, this plane becomes a nebulous (and impossible-to-visualize) m-dimensional expanse referred to as *the* **θ**-*space*. (Note that **θ** is bold, denoting that it is a vector such that $\theta = \{\theta_1, \theta_2, \ldots, \theta_m\}$, where m is the number of latent traits.) Second, while the parameters from UIRT can be directly extended to compensatory MIRT models, the same cannot be said for partially compensatory models. For now, we will focus mostly on the compensatory 2-dimensional M2PL example introduced in Chapter 3, wherein $\mathbf{a}_i = \{1.0, 0.8\}$ and $c_i = -0.2$.

The Item Response Surface

In UIRT models, discrimination parameters are proportional to the steepness of the response probability curve at its inflection point. In MIRT modeling, however, there are multiple latent traits underlying the probability of a correct response/endorsement, so rather than a response curve, we have a response surface. Figure 5.2 depicts the response surface of our hypothetical item in which the probability of a correct response is highest when the

Figure 5.2   An item response surface with parameters $\mathbf{a}_i = \{1.0, 0.8\}$ and $c_i = -0.2$, Shown from four different perspectives: 20° (i) and 40° (ii) clockwise rotations, and 70° (iii) and 130° (iv) counterclockwise rotations.

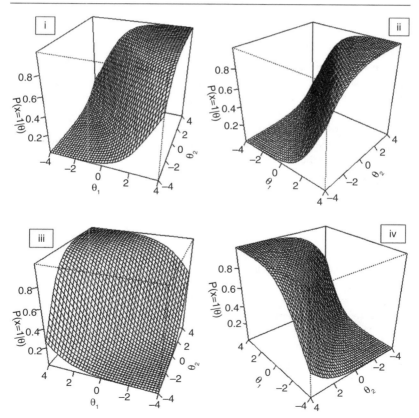

respondent excels on both of the underlying traits (θ_1 and θ_2). Because this surface is 3-dimensional, it is shown here from multiple perspectives. Plot (i) gives a typical representation of a response surface: The surface has been rotated 20° clockwise so that both latent traits are visible, though the steepness of the surface is perhaps difficult to distinguish. In plot (ii), the same surface has been rotated an additional 20° clockwise to better display how θ_1 contributes to the steepness of the surface. Plots (iii) and (iv) rotate the surface 70° and 130°, respectively, in the opposite direction in order to highlight the role of θ_2. Notice that the θ_2 scale is oriented such that lower levels of θ_2 are on the right end of the scale rather than the left. By examining this surface from multiple perspectives, it becomes clear that both θ_1 and θ_2 are helpful in discriminating between respondents of varying ability. (See the Companion Student Study Site for R code that will produce an animation of a 360° rotating 3-dimensional response surface.)

Conditional Response Functions

In addition to rotating the surface, we can also examine it by conditioning on one latent trait at a time. By taking cross-sections, or "slices," of the response surface at various points along each θ scale, we can better understand how the latent traits interact. Figure 5.3 depicts this conditional slicing. The item response function at the top displays the response probability as a function of θ_1, given that $\theta_2 = 2$ (i.e., when a slice parallel to the θ_1 axis is taken at precisely $\theta_2 = 2$). In other words, this upper panel illustrates the shape of θ_1 when the respondent is somewhat high on θ_2. The second example displays a cross-section of the surface at $\theta_2 = 0$. Here, examinees with average ability on θ_2 must have at least average ability on θ_1 if they are likely to respond correctly. Finally, the bottom panel shows the θ_1 response curve when the respondent's ability with regard to θ_2 is –2. We see that when θ_2 is low, θ_1 must be fairly high in order for the respondent to have a high correct response probability. Overall, we can think of the three conditional item response functions in terms of difficulty: As θ_2 increases from –2 to 0 to 2, it becomes "easier" (in terms of θ_1) for an examinee to provide a correct response. We could also slice the surface in the other direction so that the response probability is represented as a function of θ_2 conditional on θ_1. Doing so would reveal that a correct response is more likely when the respondent possesses strong abilities on either θ_1 or θ_2. (This relationship between dimensions demonstrates the compensatory nature of the M2PL: Low levels of θ_2 can be compensated with high levels of θ_1 and vice versa.)

Figure 5.3 An item response surface with parameters $\mathbf{a}_i = \{1.0, 0.8\}$ and $c_i = -0.2$, conditioned on θ_2 values of $+2$ (top), 0 (middle), and -2 (bottom).

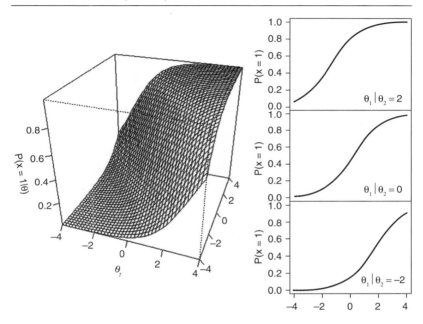

Conditional item response functions are particularly useful when trying to understand the form of a partially compensatory MIRT item. Figure 5.4 displays the item response surface of a PC M2PL model with the same parameters as in the previous figure. However, now the cross-sections do not differ in terms of difficulty; rather, they differ in terms of discrimination. The top panel, for example, has a fairly steep slope, meaning θ_1 discriminates well between low and high abilities when θ_2 is high. In the middle panel, the slope is milder, meaning θ_1 is less discriminatory when examinees are located at $\theta_2 = 0$. In the bottom panel, the curve is nearly flat; here, θ_1 adds almost nothing in terms of discriminating between low and high abilities. As in the previous example, slices could also be taken with regard to θ_1 and the results would be similar. These cross-sections reflect the partially compensatory nature of this model: The examinee must be high on both θ_1 (i.e., located somewhere in the right half of each panel) *and* θ_2 (e.g., located in the top panel) in order to have a high probability of responding correctly.

60

Figure 5.4   An item response surface with parameters $\mathbf{a}_i = \{1.0, 0.8\}$ and $\mathbf{b}_i = \{-0.2, 0.5\}$, conditioned on θ_2 values of +2 (top), 0 (middle), and –2 (bottom).

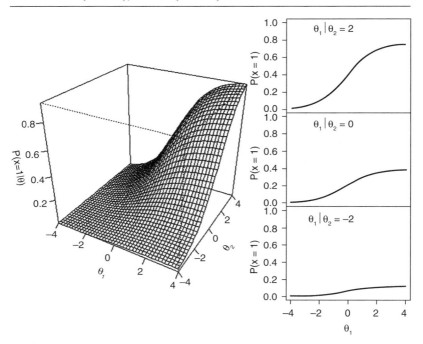

The Direction of Measurement

For the compensatory M2PL model, imagine that an item's response surface is a piece of paper that has been bent into an S-shape (also known as an *ogive*). One latent trait may have a greater impact on the probability of a correct response to this particular item, so this S-shaped paper needs to be rotated accordingly. For instance, if θ_1 plays a larger role than θ_2 in the probability of correct response, then the paper should be rotated toward θ_1. Consider the four contour plots shown in Figure 5.5. As discussed in the previous chapter, you can think of these contour plots as the view you would have when looking down through the surface onto the θ-plane. Here, we add three graphical elements that will assist us in comprehending the shape and orientation of the response surface. The first is a bolded contour line, which represents the combinations of θ_1 and θ_2 that are associated with a $P = 0.5$ probability of correct response (i.e., the same threshold used in

defining the difficulty parameter in the unidimensional 2PL model presented in Chapter 2). The second is a dotted line indicating the axis along
which the surface is oriented, which Muraki and Carlson (1995) termed the
direction of measurement. The third is an arrow, pointing in the direction of
measurement, whose length reflects the steepness of the surface such that
longer arrows are indicative of steeper surfaces. We will return to slope
steepness later.

The four contours in Figure 5.5 reflect items with equal difficulty. In
each plot, the first discrimination parameter a_1 is fixed at 1.0, but a_2 varies.
Plot (i) presents the contours when $a_2 = 0.1$. Here, the second dimension
hardly discriminates at all and thus barely plays a role in the probability of

Figure 5.5 Contour plots for four items of equal difficulty. In all four
panels, the first discrimination parameter $a_1 = 1.0$. The
second discrimination parameter $a_2 = 0.1, 0.5, 1.0$, and 2.0
for plots (i), (ii), (iii), and (iv), respectively.

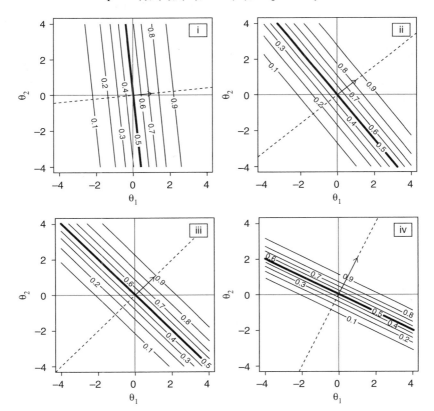

correct response. Accordingly, the direction of measurement basically follows the θ_1 scale because θ_2 is not contributing to the response probability (meaning this may actually be a unidimensional item). In plot (ii), $a_2 = 0.5$. Now the second dimension plays more of a role, and though the second dimension is fairly weak in terms of discrimination, the angle of the direction of measurement has shifted away from the θ_1 scale. In plot (iii), $a_2 = 1.0$, meaning latent traits 1 and 2 are equally involved in the probability of providing a correct response. We can also see in this panel that the probability lines are closer together and the arrow is longer, meaning the response surface is steeper than in the previous panels. Finally, in plot (iv), $a_2 = 2.0$, and thus, the direction of measurement is oriented more toward the second dimension than the first. In addition, the probability contour lines in this final plot are quite close together and the arrow is long, thereby signifying the increased slope of this surface. The overall takeaway of Figure 5.5 is that item discrimination in MIRT models affects not only the steepness of the surface but also the direction of measurement. When interpreting MIRT parameters and describing the results, it is important that we keep in mind the direction of measurement and the role of the $\mathbf{a}_i$ parameters in defining that direction.

Aside from eyeballing the shape of the M2PL response surface, we can also quantify the degree of rotation, the distance and direction from the origin, and the steepness of the slope. The degree (literally) to which the surface has been rotated can be found using a bit of trigonometry. Recall

Figure 5.6   Geometric relationships between item discrimination
parameters in a 2-dimensional MIRT model.

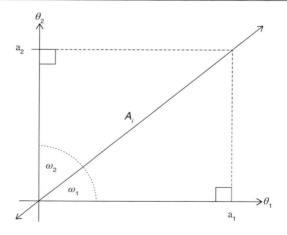

Pythagoras's theorem for computing the length of the hypotenuse of a right triangle: $\text{Side1}^2 + \text{Side2}^2 = \text{hypotenuse}^2$. In the M2PL case, we can think of Side1 as a_1 (the discrimination parameter relative to θ_1) and Side2 as a_2 (the discrimination parameter relative to θ_2), as shown in Figure 5.6. We can then find the hypotenuse of the right triangle in the figure by solving for A_i in the formula $a_1^2 + a_2^2 = A_i^2$.

For example, if one dimension has a discrimination parameter of $a_1 = 1.0$ and the other has a discrimination parameter of $a_2 = 0.8$, then the hypotenuse A_i is equal to $\sqrt{a_1^2 + a_2^2} = \sqrt{1.64} = 1.28$. More generally, A_i is known as the *multidimensional discrimination index* (occasionally referenced in the literature as *MDISC*):

$$A_i = \sqrt{\sum_{m=1}^{M} a_{im}^2}. \tag{5.1}$$

That is, the multidimensional discrimination index is the square root of the sum of squared discrimination parameters for each of the latent traits underlying correct response/endorsement.

Conceptually, the multidimensional A_i parameter is analogous to the unidimensional a parameter and can be interpreted similarly: Higher A_i values indicate an item response surface that discriminates well between low and high levels of the latent traits. However, there is an important distinction, which once again relates to the θ-space. A_i is proportional to the slope of the surface at the point of steepest slope *in a particular direction* from the origin of the θ-space. Once we know the length of the sides and hypotenuse of our right triangle, we can use standard trigonometry to compute ω_1—the angle formed by a_1 and A_i in the figure. We can find this angle by determining the cosine:

$$\cos \omega_1 = \frac{a_1}{A_i}. \tag{5.2}$$

Cosines are the ratio of the adjacent side to the hypotenuse, which is precisely what we see here: The numerator is the adjacent side of our angle, based on the item discrimination parameters in $\mathbf{a}_i$, while the denominator is the root sum of the squared discrimination parameters (i.e., the hypotenuse A_i). We can take the arc cosine of this value to obtain the angle relative to the coordinate axes. For example, the direction from the origin to the point of steepest slope, relative to latent trait $m = 1$, is found by

$$\omega_1 = \arccos\left(\frac{a_1}{A}\right). \tag{5.3}$$

This will return a value in radians, which can be converted to degrees by multiplying the result by $180/\pi$. Plugging in the values from our example item produces an angle of

$$\omega_1 = \arccos\left(\frac{1}{\sqrt{.1^2 + 0.8^2}}\right) \times \left(\frac{180}{\pi}\right) = 38.66°$$

relative to the axis of dimension $m = 1$. Angle ω_2 in Figure 5.6 is given by

$$\omega_2 = \arccos\left(\frac{0.8}{\sqrt{1^2 + 0.8^2}}\right) \times \left(\frac{180}{\pi}\right) = 51.34°.$$

Note that these two angles sum to 90°; that is, in the 2-dimensional case, the angle relative to the first latent trait axis is the complement of the angle relative to the second latent trait axis.

For m-dimensional MIRT models in general, we can use Equation (5.2) to determine a vector of angles $\boldsymbol{\omega}_m$ for each item (e.g., $\boldsymbol{\omega}_m$ in our example item would represent both ω_1 [38.66°] and ω_2 [51.34°]). These *direction cosines* indicate the direction from the origin of the $\boldsymbol{\theta}$-space to the point at which the response surface has the steepest slope. When there are m dimensions, $\boldsymbol{\omega}_m$ will include $m - 1$ direction cosines.

Based on Equations (5.1) and (5.2), we now know the multidimensional discrimination index and the direction of measurement. We can also compute a *multidimensional difficulty index* (sometimes referred to as *MDIFF*). In the 2-dimensional example, the origin of the $\boldsymbol{\theta}$-space represents average difficulty/ability with regard to *both* latent traits. Difficulty/ability is then inferred relative to the origin, just as in UIRT. However, because we are working with a plane instead of a line, the distance from the origin can be in any direction. As we observed in the contour plots earlier, the individual a_i parameters orient the response surface in a quantifiable way around the origin, meaning that A_i, which is obtained from the individual a_i parameters, includes information about the direction of measurement. Thus, difficulty in compensatory MIRT models is defined as

$$B_i = \frac{\sum_{m=1}^{M} \mathbf{a}_i' \mathbf{b}_i}{A_i} = \frac{-c_i}{A_i}, \tag{5.4}$$

where c_i is the intercept term from the MIRT model and A_i is the multidimensional discrimination index as described above. The multidimensional B_i parameter is interpreted just as the unidimensional b_i parameter: Items with high values of B_i require high levels of θ in order to have a high likelihood of correct response. Again, however, this interpretation is only accurate in a specific direction.

To gain a deeper understanding of the multidimensional difficulty index, consider the four contour plots presented in Figure 5.7. Each plot displays the compensatory M2PL contour lines for an item with discrimination parameters $a_i = \{1.0, 0.8\}$. As before, the bold contour line represents the $P = 0.5$ probability of correct response, the dotted line represents the axis of measurement, and the arrow represents the multidimensional discrimination of the item. However, the plots shown here vary in terms of difficulty. Plot (i), for example, displays the contours of an item with difficulty parameters $b_i = \{-2, 1\}$; the intersection of these b_i parameters is indicated by the + in the upper left quadrant. Notice that item difficulty is still associated with $P = 0.5$, just as in the unidimensional 2PL model. In fact, it is the difficulty parameters that dictate precisely where the $P = 0.5$ diagonal lies within the θ-space.

Figure 5.7   Contour plots for four items of equal discrimination but varying difficulty. In all four panels, the discrimination parameters in $a_i = \{1.0, 0.8\}$. The difficulty parameters in $b_i = (-2, 1), (2, 1), (-2, -1),$ and $(2, -1)$, as indicated by the + in plots (i), (ii), (iii), and (iv), respectively.

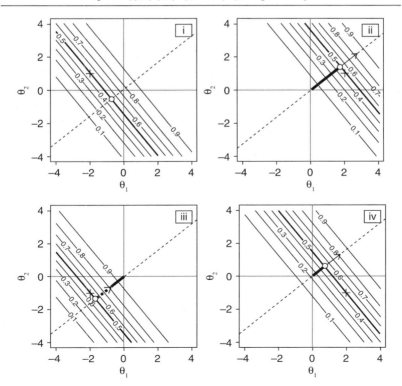

To visualize the multidimensional difficulty index, we need to take the direction of measurement into consideration. More specifically, M2PL difficulty is defined as the distance along the axis of measurement (as determined by the discrimination parameters in $\mathbf{a}_i$) from the origin to the $P = 0.5$ contour (as determined by the difficulty parameters in the intercept term c_i). In Figure 5.6, this distance is the length of the bold line segment that extends from the origin to the white dot on the $P = 0.5$ contour. In plot (i), the length of this segment is found by

$$B_i = \frac{(1*-2)+(0.8*1)}{\sqrt{1^2+0.8^2}} = -0.937.$$

This negative multidimensional difficulty value indicates that the white dot is to the left of the origin (i.e., that this is a relatively easy item).

In plot (ii), the individual difficulty parameters $\mathbf{b}_{ii} = \{2, 1\}$, as denoted by the $+$ in the upper right quadrant, result in intercept parameter $c_{ii} = -2.8$. The multidimensional difficulty index, represented again by the bold line segment from the origin to the white dot, is $B_{ii} = 2.8/1.28 = 2.186$. Working through the other plots will reveal $B_{iii} = -2.186$, and $B_{iv} = .937$. Thus, of the four items shown in these plots, item (ii) is the most difficult, followed by items (iv), (i), and (iii). This ranking can also be seen by noting the placement of the white dot along the axis of measurement in each plot. When this dot is farther to the right (relative to the axis of measurement), then the item can be considered more difficult. It is especially important to keep in mind the direction of measurement when making relative comparisons between the B parameters of a set of items: A B of, say, 1.5 in a particular direction may be meaningfully different from a B of 1.5 in a different direction.

To put it all together, Muraki and Carlson (1995) noted that the cross-section of a 2-dimensional item response surface along the direction of measurement will yield a unidimensional item response function with a discrimination parameter equal to A_i and a difficulty parameter equal to B_i. This cross-section is visualized in Figure 5.8, where the item response surface is a compensatory M2PL model with parameters $\mathbf{a}_i = \{1.0, 0.8\}$ and $c_i = -0.2$. The $P = 0.5$ contour line and discrimination arrow are superimposed onto the floor of this figure to show the direction of measurement and the distance from the origin. The 2-dimensional slice falls on the axis of measurement, thereby producing a unidimensional 2PL item response function with parameters $a = A = \sqrt{a_1^2 + a_2^2} = 1.28$ and $b = B = \dfrac{-c}{A_i} = .156$.

67

Figure 5.8 An M2PL item response surface and the cross-section taken along its direction of measurement. Both the surface and the cross-section have parameters of $A_i = 1.28$ and $B_i = 0.156$.

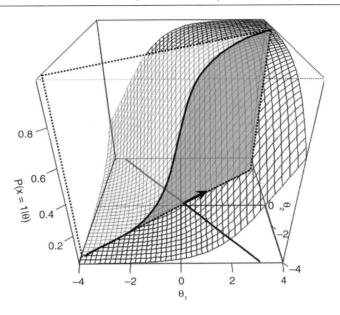

Person Parameters in MIRT

The multidimensional discrimination and difficulty indexes presented earlier are, of course, item characteristics. Once we know the distance and direction from the origin to the coordinates of interest, we can use these trigonometric relationships to find *person* parameters. More specifically, we can use the direction of measurement to reckon the location of θ along each dimension m for a particular person p:

$$\theta_m = \zeta_p \cos \omega_m, \tag{5.5}$$

where ζ_p is the distance of person p from the origin of the θ-space and ω_m is the angle relative to dimension m. In the 2-dimensional case, this formula simply says that a person's location relative to the given dimension is located a certain distance from (0, 0) in a particular direction. Conceptually, this is not dissimilar from UIRT, wherein a person's location along the single dimension is a certain distance from zero in a particular (positive or negative) direction.

Equation (5.5) can be used to take cross-sections of the multidimensional surface in any direction, just as depicted in Figure 5.8. Essentially, each slice of the MIRT surface can then be interpreted and quantified within the more familiar context of UIRT modeling. For instance, the height of the response surface, meaning the correct response probability curve, at any location in the θ-space can be found by replacing the θ values from the MIRT model with the distance and angle values from the right side of Equation (5.5). The M2PL model (Equation [3.1]), for example, would then become

$$P\left(x_{ip} = 1 \mid \boldsymbol{\omega}_p, \zeta_p; \mathbf{a}_i, c_i\right) = \frac{\exp\left[\left(\zeta_p \sum_{m=1}^{M} a_{im} \cos \omega_{pm}\right) + c_i\right]}{1 + \exp\left[\left(\zeta_p \sum_{m=1}^{M} a_{im} \cos \omega_{pm}\right) + c_i\right]}, \qquad (5.6)$$

where ζ_p is placed outside the summation sign since it is a scalar. In summary, Equation (5.6) will provide the probability of correct response relative to a respondent's location, as defined by the distance and direction inherent in the θ coordinates.

We can also use Equation (5.5), and a bit of calculus, to determine the slope (i.e., the discrimination parameter of the cross-section) of the item response surface in any direction from the $\boldsymbol{\theta}$-space. The first derivative of a curve represents the slope of the tangent line at any point along that curve. The partial derivative of Equation (5.6) with respect to the person scalar ζ_p provides the slope of the M2PL item response surface in a particular direction ω_{pm}:

$$\frac{\partial P\left(x_{ip} = 1 \mid \boldsymbol{\omega}_p, \zeta_p; \mathbf{a}_i, c_i\right)}{\partial \zeta_p} = P_{ip} Q_{ip} \sum_{m=1}^{M} a_{im} \cos \omega_{pm}, \qquad (5.7)$$

where P_{ip} and Q_{ip} are abbreviations for the probability of correct and incorrect response, respectively, for person p on item i. The intercept term C_i is a constant and therefore drops out of the equation, leaving the slope of the response surface to depend on the probability of a correct response, the item discrimination parameters in $\mathbf{a}_i$, and the direction indicated by the angles in $\boldsymbol{\omega}_p$ While the discrimination parameters would be estimated by the model, the angles could be adjusted by the researcher, thereby helping make sense of the shape of the response surface. Note that if we plug in our hypothetical discrimination parameter values $\mathbf{a}_i = \{1.0, 0.8\}$, we can determine the slope in any direction we wish to investigate. We could explore, for example, an angle such as $\omega_p = \{5.00°, 85.00°\}$, which corresponds to a direction that strongly favors the first dimension. The slope in this direction is then $\sum_{m=1}^{M} a_{im} \cos \omega_{pm} = (1.0 \times \cos 5.00°) + (0.8 \times \cos 85.00°) = (1.0 \times .996) + (0.8 \times .087) = 1.066$. Note that this is a milder slope than we previously established along our optimal direction of measurement $\omega_p = \{38.66°, 51.34°\}$: $\sum_{m=1}^{M} a_{im} \cos \omega_{pm} = (1.0 \times \cos 38.66°) + (0.8 \times \cos 51.34°) = (1.0 \times .781) + (0.8 \times .625) = 1.28$ (i.e., the multidimensional discrimination index A_i that we calculated earlier).

We can also use calculus to identify, for any user-specified direction, the precise location in the θ-space at which the item response surface is steepest (i.e., the difficulty parameter of the cross-section). The second derivative of Equation (5.6) with respect to ζ_p can be used to identify the precise location in the θ-space at which the slope of the item response surface is steepest:

$$\frac{\partial^2 P\left(x_{ip} = 1 \mid \boldsymbol{\omega}_p, \zeta_p; \mathbf{a}_i, c_i\right)}{\partial \zeta_p^2} = \left(\sum_{m=1}^{M} a_{im} \cos \omega_{pm}\right)^2 P_{ip}\left(1 - 3P_{ip} + 2P_{ip}^2\right). \qquad (5.8)$$

The exact point of steepest slope is determined by setting the right side (and specifically the rightmost term) of Equation (5.8) to zero: $P_{ip}(1 - 3P_{ip} + 2P_{ip}^2) = 0$. Factoring the term in parentheses gives $P_{ip}(2P_{ip} - 1)(P_{ip} - 1) = 0$, which offers three solutions: $P_{ip} = \{0, 0.5, 1\}$. By definition, $P_{ip} = 0$ when $\zeta_p = -\infty$ and $P_{ip} = 1$ when $\zeta_p = +\infty$, so of these three solutions, only $P_{ip} = 0.5$ gives a finite value of ζ_p. Thus, we need to determine the value of ζ_p that will produce $P_{ip} = 0.5$. Recall that P_{is} is shorthand for the probability of correct response, which in this case is obtained from the M2PL item response function in Equation (5.6), which contains the person scalar ζ_p. We can find this value quite easily by recognizing that when the exponent in the M2PL function equals zero, then $P_{ip} = \dfrac{e^0}{1+e^0} = \dfrac{1}{1+1} = 0.5$. So now we just need to find the value of ζ_p that will set the exponent in the M2PL function to zero:

$$\left(\zeta_p \sum_{m=1}^{M} a_{im} \cos \omega_{pm}\right) + c_i = 0$$

$$\zeta_p = \frac{-c_i}{\sum_{m=1}^{M} a_{im} \cos \omega_{pm}}.$$ (5.9)

In summary, Equation (5.9) provides the distance along a line, in any direction specified by the angles in ω_p, at which the item response surface is steepest. Note that by plugging in the angles that define our optimal direction of measurement, we will obtain the multidimensional difficulty index B_i:

$$\zeta_p = \frac{-(-.2)}{(1.0 \times \cos 38.66°) + (0.8 \times \cos 51.34°)}$$

$$= \frac{.2}{(1.0 \times .781) + (0.8 \times .625)} = .156$$

MIRT Information

Another important aspect of a MIRT analysis is the information function, which describes the region of the θ-space in which measurement of the person parameters is most precise. Recall that in UIRT, 2PL information is the square of the discrimination parameter times the variance PQ, where P is the probability of correct response and Q is the probability of incorrect response (i.e., $1 - P$). Information is defined similarly in MIRT, though, of course, we have to consider the direction of measurement. Conveniently, the multidimensional discrimination parameter A_i incorporates the direction of the steepest slope. The M2PL information function in the direction of steepest slope is then given by

$$I(\theta) = P(\theta) Q(\theta) A^2,$$ (5.10)

which is conceptually identical to the 2PL information function.

The information surface and contour plot for our example M2PL item are shown in Figure 5.9. This item is most informative, meaning it provides the most precise measure of examinees' true abilities, along the diagonal from $(-2.5, 4.0)$ to $(3.5, -4.0)$ in the θ-space. The standard error of measurement, which reflects the accuracy of the θ estimate, is proportional to the inverse of the information function, so it would be smallest across this diagonal. The contour plot also reveals that this item is not at all informative for respondents in the lower and upper triangles that are bounded by the $I = .05$ contour line. That is, this particular item is not going to provide meaningful information about the true abilities of examinees who are either high on both dimensions or low on both dimensions.

Figure 5.9 Information surface (left) and contour plot (right) of a compensatory M2PL model with parameters $\mathbf{a}_i = \{1.0, 0.8\}$ and $c_i = -0.2$.

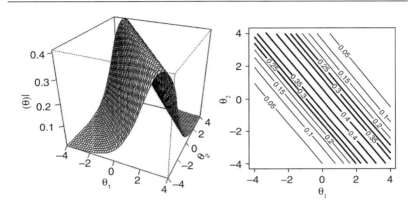

We can also use Equation (5.10) with partially compensatory MIRT models. The formula stays the same, but the response surface and contour lines shown in Figure 5.10 look much different because of the multiplicative nature of the PC M2PL model. Here, the surface and contours are peaked across a curved rather than diagonal range. Specifically, information in this PC M2PL model is maximized between the $I = 0.4$ contours, which cover a region of the θ-space that curves from (0.2, 4.0) to (4.0, 0.2). The lower left portion of the θ-space reflects that the PC M2PL model does not provide informative measurement for individuals who are low on either θ_1 or θ_2.

Polytomous MIRT Descriptives

All the M2PL descriptive statistics described earlier apply to polytomous MIRT models as well. That is, polytomous MIRT models produce complex category response surfaces that are oriented in a particular direction and at a certain distance from the origin of the θ-space. To better understand the effects of multidimensionality on the GRM, for example, we can examine the conditional item response functions. Figure 5.11 displays the MGRM category response surfaces presented in Chapter 4; here, we see the conditional cross-sections at $\theta_2 = +2, 0$, and -2. Examining these slices will help us make sense of the unintuitive surface plot. For instance, the top panel shows that when θ_2 is high, response category $k = 1$ (the solid line) is only the most likely choice when the respondent is low (<-1.5) on the θ_1 scale.

72

Figure 5.10 Information surface (left) and contour plot (right) of a partially compensatory M2PL model with parameters $\mathbf{a}_i = \{1.0, 0.8\}$ and $\mathbf{b}_i = \{-0.2, 0.5\}$.

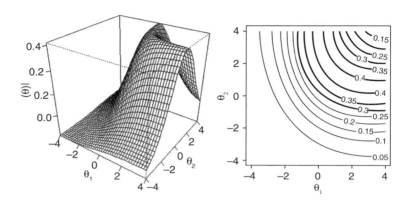

Figure 5.11 Category response surfaces of an MGRM response function with parameters $\mathbf{a}_i = \{1, 1.5\}$ and $\mathbf{\tau}_i = \{-.25, .75\}$, conditions on θ_2 values of +2 (top), 0 (middle), and −2 (bottom).

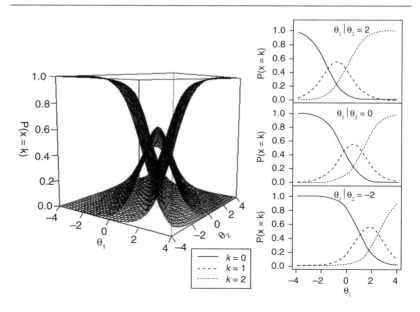

Similarly, the bottom panel shows that when examinees are low on θ_2, then response category 3 is only likely when θ_1 is very high (>3.0). In terms of the example social situation enjoyment item from Chapter 4, these conditional cross-sections tell us that regardless of anxiety (θ_1) level, an examinee is unlikely to select "*Always*" (i.e., $k = 0$) if she is highly introverted (e.g., $\theta_2 = 2$) or "*Never*" (i.e., $k = 2$) if she is highly extroverted (e.g., $\theta_2 = -2$). Again, slices could be cut perpendicular to the θ_1 axis and similar conclusions would be drawn (and the supplemental material to this text includes R code that will allow you to condition on any values of interest).

One descriptive tool that is unique to polytomous models is the expected item response score, meaning the observed response that we would expect to see given the respondent's location in the θ-space. In dichotomous models, of course, there are only two scores, so the idea of an expected score is redundant. But when there are multiple scores (i.e., $k = 0$, 1, or 2), then it may be useful to examine the expected score in addition to the probability of selecting a certain response. Figure 5.12 illustrates the surface and contours of the expected item score function for our example item. Notice that the z-axis in the panel on the left now represents the expected score (which ranges from 0 to 2) for our three category items, rather than the response probability (which ranges from 0 to 1). In terms of the social situations example, where θ_1 is anxiety and θ_2 is introversion, these plots reveal that individuals who are high in anxiety ($\theta_1 = 2$) but low in

Figure 5.12 Expected item score surface (left) and contour plot (right) of an MGRM response function with parameters $\mathbf{a}_i = \{1, 1.5\}$ and $\mathbf{\tau}_i = \{-.25, .75\}$.

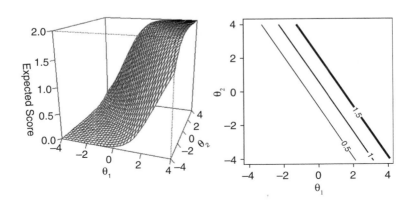

introversion ($\theta_2 = -2$), for example, are expected to select response category 1 (*Sometimes*; i.e., provide a score of 1), while those who have average levels of anxiety ($\theta_1 = 0$) but are highly extroverted ($\theta_2 = 3$) are expected to select category 2 (*Never*). The compensatory nature of the MGRM is also shown in Figure 5.12: When individuals possess high levels of both θ_{anx} and θ_{int}, it is highly probable that they will select category 2 (*Never*).

Finally, we will examine the item information function of the MGRM. While dichotomous information surfaces are, by definition, unimodal, polytomous information surfaces may have up to $k-1$ peaks. We see the slightly bimodal information surface of our example item in Figure 5.13. Note that the z-axis is information $I(\theta)$ rather than probability, and the maximum information in the direction of measurement actually occurs at $I(\theta) = 1.93$. We can see that the surface slopes steeply to the first peak, then there is a slight shallow dip, a second peak, and then a steep descent. This topography suggests that our example item is fairly informative across a sizable region of the θ-space, including not only the peaks but also the narrow plateau between them. We can get a better sense of the information function by inspecting the contour plot. The wide white swath in the middle of the contour plot represents the plateau associated with θ values along the diagonal from $(-2.0, 4.0)$ to $(3.0, -4.0)$. Overall, then, this item provides accurate measurement of the person parameters across a considerable region of the θ-space, covering many combinations of anxiety and introversion.

Figure 5.13   Information surface (left) and contour plot (right) of an MGRM response function with parameters $\mathbf{a}_i = \{1, 1.5\}$ and $\mathbf{\tau}_i = \{-.25, .75\}$.

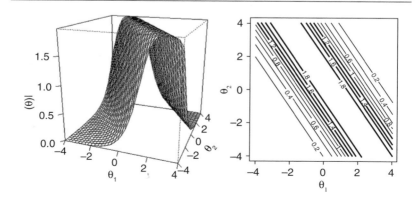

Test-Level MIRT Descriptives

So far, we have focused on individual items, but several of the descriptions of item functioning can be extended to describe the psychometric properties of an entire test. For example, we can produce a *test characteristic surface* by simply summing the individual item response surfaces:

$$E\left(y_p \mid \boldsymbol{\theta}_p\right) = \sum_{i=1}^{n} P\left(x_{ip} \mid \boldsymbol{\theta}_p\right),$$

where the total score y_p is found by summing the response functions $P(.)$ across all n items on the test. $P(.)$ can be a dichotomous or polytomous function or a mixture of both item types. The result will resemble the expected polytomous item score presented in Figure 5.12. That is, it will be a monotonically increasing surface, where the lowest score ($y_p = 0$) will be associated with low levels of each latent trait and the highest score ($y_p = n*k_i$, where k_i is the number of response categories) will be associated with the highest levels of each latent trait. Test information functions can also be found by summing across the individual item information functions as described earlier, and the resulting surface is interpreted similarly. We will not go further into MIRT test functioning here, but interested readers should consult Ackerman (1996) and Reckase (2009), who provide several additional descriptions of item and test functioning in MIRT models, including comparisons of unidimensional and multidimensional θ estimates, centroid plots that compare summed scores and MIRT-scaled θ scores, and clamshell plots that provide further details regarding the direction of measurement.

Chapter 6

ITEM FACTOR STRUCTURES

Thus far, we have examined a number of multidimensional item-level models. We turn now to test-level models. It is not uncommon to see the general term *MIRT model* being used in reference to the full test rather than the individual items. Here, we distinguish between item-level MIRT models (such as the M2PL or MGRM from Chapters 3 and 4) and what we will refer to as *item factor structures*. These test-level models characterize the overall structure of a test—the number of latent dimensions and their associations with one another and with each item (Bock, Gibbons, & Muraki, 1988)—just as in factor analysis or structural equation modeling. Most of the common item factor structures can be considered in the context of the two-tier item factor analysis model (L. Cai, 2010b), which will frame our discussion.

Two-Tier Model

Consider a reading comprehension exam in which test-takers must read four literary passages and answer sets of corresponding items. Items 1 through 3 are related to an excerpt from *Moby Dick*, Items 4 through 6 are related to an excerpt from *Don Quixote*, Items 7 through 9 are related to a poem by T. S. Eliot, and Items 10 through 12 are related to a poem by Emily Dickinson. Different hypotheses could be made regarding the structure of this test. It could be that certain test-takers have a strong grasp of literary prose, but they struggle with comprehending poetry, in which case it would make sense to specify two dimensions (one for prose and one for poetry). However, the clustering of item content would violate the local independence assumption, thereby necessitating four separate dimensions (one for each excerpt). The two-tier model allows us to incorporate both of these hypotheses by specifying an item factor structure with two primary dimensions in the first tier and four secondary dimensions in the second tier.

Figure 6.1 presents a diagram of our two-tier model of reading comprehension. Following standard factor analytic diagramming conventions, the squares represent observed variables (i.e., the item responses), the large circles represent the latent variables on the primary tier (i.e., prose comprehension and poetry comprehension), and the small circles represent the latent variables on the secondary tier (i.e., the item clusters related to each passage). The double-headed curved arrow

78

Figure 6.1   Factor diagram of the two-tier model.

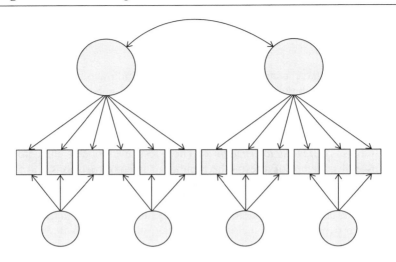

indicates the relationship between primary dimensions, while the single-headed straight arrows indicate the relationships between the latent and observed variables.

We can further examine the two-tier model by considering its formulation with regard to the M2PL model:

$$P\left(x_{ip} = 1 \mid \boldsymbol{\eta}_i, \xi_{is}, \Psi\right) = \frac{1}{1 + \exp\left\{-\left[c_i\left(\Psi\right) + \left[\mathbf{a}_i\left(\Psi\right)\right]' \boldsymbol{\eta}_i + a_{is}\left(\Psi\right)\xi_{is}\right]\right\}}, \quad (6.1)$$

where c_i is the intercept, $\mathbf{a}_i$ is a vector of item discrimination parameters on the primary factors in vector $\boldsymbol{\eta}_i$, a_{is} is the item discrimination parameter on the secondary factor ξ_{is}, and $\boldsymbol{\psi}$ represents all estimable and/or structural parameters in the model. The term within the braces shows that the item parameters (the M2PL intercept and discrimination parameters in this case) depend on the overall structure of the two-tier model, as denoted by $\boldsymbol{\psi}$. Although Equation (6.1) presents the two-tier structure in the context of an M2PL model, it can also be implemented using polytomously scored items (see Cai, 2010b, for two-tier adaptations of the graded and nominal response models).

The two-tier model offers several advantages. First, it is a relatively flexible model: It allows for any number or arrangement of dimensions in

79

the primary tier (subject to identification) as well as cross-loadings across the primary dimensions. Second, L. Cai (2010b) demonstrated that EAP scores from the two-tier model are more precise due to the "borrowing of strength" among the primary dimensions. That is, the scoring accuracy on one primary dimension is enhanced because of statistical information that is supplied by the other primary dimensions. Third, the two-tier model permits a number of interesting applications, including longitudinal analyses, evaluation of randomized controlled trial data, detection of response styles, and more. A few of these applications are presented in Chapter 9.

Bonifay (2015) presents an illustration of the two-tier model using data from a high-dimensional screening questionnaire for psychiatric diagnosis. More specifically, this chapter presents a two-tier analysis of a 139-item screener that measures 13 Axis I psychiatric disorders. The first tier comprised two correlated primary factors representing overall psychiatric impairment and major depressive disorder. The second tier comprised 19 additional factors; 7 of these secondary factors were related to the depression factor, while the remaining 12 were associated with the general psychiatric impairment variable. Although this arrangement was exceedingly complex, the results demonstrated that the two-tier structure essentially eliminated the problematic levels of local dependence that were found in simpler MIRT analyses.

Figure 6.2   Alternate item factor structures within the two-tier model.

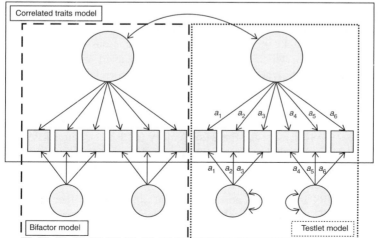

As mentioned at the beginning of this section, several popular models are nested within, or closely related to, the flexible two-tier model; in other words, by eliminating specific arrows and variables from the two-tier diagram, we can produce a number of familiar models. Figure 6.2 demonstrates how the two-tier model encompasses two of the most widely used structures—the correlated-traits and bifactor models—and is closely related to the testlet response model. A correlated-traits model can be constructed by focusing only on the correlated primary dimensions, a bifactor model can be constructed by focusing on a single primary dimension and its associated secondary dimensions, and a testlet response model is similar to a bifactor model but with equality constraints between the primary and secondary factor loadings of each item and freely estimated secondary factor variances. We will briefly review each of these models in turn.

Correlated-Traits Model

Perhaps the most fundamental item factor structure is the correlated-traits model. As its name implies, this model includes multiple related latent traits (as seen in the primary tier of the two-tier model). This correlated-traits structure has long been a fixture in MIRT modeling, especially in the early days when the estimation problems of more complex structures had not yet been solved. Indeed, the chapter-length discussion on test structures in Reckase's (2009) seminal MIRT textbook focuses only on correlated-traits models. However, this relatively simple structure is no longer the only choice for MIRT modelers, thanks to gains in computing efficiency and advances in the estimation of complex latent variable models (see Chapter 7). Some authors (e.g., Adams et al., 1997) distinguish between-item multidimensionality (in which each item is associated with just one of the multiple latent traits that make up the item factor structure) from within-item multidimensionality (in which each item may be associated with more than one latent trait). As shown in Figure 6.2, only the correlated-traits structure facilitates the modeling of between-item multidimensionality.

An especially accessible illustration of the correlated-traits model is presented by L. Cai and Hansen (2017) in the context of the English Language Proficiency Assessment for the 21st Century (ELPA21). The ELPA21 is a large-scale educational assessment that was designed to measure the four content domains of listening, speaking, reading, and writing. In this brief paper, the authors discuss the statistical and practical advantages of fitting a single MIRT model with correlated latent dimensions rather than fitting separate UIRT models for each domain. A more technical example is provided by Brown and Maydeu-Olivares (2011) in their MIRT analysis of the Big Five personality factors.

Bifactor Model

The bifactor model (Holzinger & Swineford, 1937) is a factor structure that includes a single primary dimension (often called the "general factor") and multiple secondary dimensions (known as "specific factors" or "group factors"). In psychological and educational assessment, the primary dimension typically represents the main construct being measured by the test, while the secondary dimensions usually represent narrow subconstructs defined by groupings of items with similar content. A psychiatric screening questionnaire, for instance, might measure overall depression (the primary dimension) by including clusters of questions about mood, sleeping habits, diet, and so forth (the secondary dimensions; see Bonifay, 2015, for an illustration).

The bifactor model has become increasingly popular in recent years, due in part to the development of the "dimension reduction" method of efficiently estimating all the parameters in this complex structure (Gibbons & Hedeker, 1992). There have been countless bifactor modeling applications across the educational and psychological sciences and beyond. Despite (or perhaps because of) its popularity, the bifactor model has become somewhat controversial for a number of reasons (Bonifay, Lane, & Reise, 2017). One concern is the difficulty in interpreting the primary and secondary dimensions, which the model requires to be orthogonal, or independent; how should one interpret orthogonal factor scores that are based on the same item(s)? Furthermore, the bifactor model appears to possess an undesirable tendency to fit well to almost any possible data pattern (Bonifay & Cai, 2017). Accordingly, Rodriguez, Reise, and Haviland (2016) provide several statistics that can help researchers decide whether bifactor modeling is a reasonable approach. Third, this model is often selected not because of its alignment with a given theory, but due to its seemingly superior psychometric properties. As Thomas (2012) cautioned, "indiscriminate use of the bifactor model without proper regard for theory is highly questionable. . . . Simply put, the bifactor model's added benefit may not excuse its complexity" (p. 108).

The bifactor model has become exceedingly popular in recent years (Reise, 2012), and many empirical examples abound; interested readers can examine bifactor MIRT models in research contexts ranging from psychiatric disorders (Gibbons, Rush, & Immekus, 2009; Simms, Grös, Watson, & O'Hara, 2008) and nursing knowledge (Y. Cai, 2015) to civil responsibility (DeMars, 2013) and a host of others.

Testlet Response Model

Bradlow, Wainer, and Wang (1999) proposed the testlet response model for handling the data from tests that include aggregations of items that are all related to the same prompt (i.e., testlets). Structurally, the testlet model resembles the bifactor model, as illustrated in Figure 6.2: Both models include a single primary dimension and a set of secondary dimensions. In fact, the testlet model can be thought of as a bifactor model in which the specific dimension loadings within each testlet have been constrained to be proportional to the primary dimension loadings and the specific factor variances have been freed (Li, Bolt, & Fu, 2006). (Note that the freeing of these variances means that the testlet model is not formally nested within the two-tier structure.)

The testlet model would be an appropriate choice for modeling the response data from our reading comprehension exam. The items within each passage are likely to be interrelated beyond their relationship to the latent trait; in other words, the testlet items, by design, are expected to violate the local independence assumption. In the testlet response model, the secondary dimensions (known as testlet factors) are statistical random effects that capture the residual correlations within each testlet. Thus, the testlet model statistically accounts for the local item dependencies that have been intentionally built into the test design.

A recent empirical example of the testlet structure is given by Li, Li, and Wang (2010) regarding a reading comprehension exam. In this study, the reading test under investigation included three written passages and 13 to14 comprehension items about each passage. The authors demonstrate how to interpret the item parameters and fit statistics of the testlet model relative to a unidimensional model that ignores the inbuilt local dependence of the exam. Additional applications and examples of the testlet response model can be found in the aforementioned book by Bradlow et al. (1999).

R Code

The two-tier model and its associated item factor structures can be estimated in mirt using the `bfactor()` command. This command works just like the `mirt()` command we saw earlier, but the model argument is much more complex. For bifactor models, the user must indicate the specific factor that is associated with each item. For a six-item test with two specific factors, for example, the code `model = c(1, 1, 1, 2, 2, 2)` would indicate that the first three items load on specific factor 1 and the last three items load on specific factor 2. The `bfactor()` command will then estimate a bifactor model with one general factor and two specific factors. To estimate a two-tier model, the user must specify the number of primary dimensions via the `model2` argument.

Chapter 7

ESTIMATION IN MIRT MODELS

In Chapter 2, we reviewed the estimation of person and item parameters in the context of UIRT modeling. At the most basic level, estimation in MIRT is conceptually similar to estimation in UIRT: The goal is to identify the most likely item and person parameters given some observed pattern of responses. As you may have guessed, however, parameter estimation in MIRT modeling is a far more arduous task. Indeed, multidimensionality drastically complicates the estimation process, and it is only recently, thanks to numerous advancements in statistical methodology and computing power, that we have been able to efficiently estimate MIRT model parameters. While this is certainly the most complex topic in this book, the intention is to provide a relatively general overview of modern MIRT estimation methods, and to provide resources for those who would like to gain a deeper understanding of this important topic.

Conceptual Illustration

It is helpful to begin with an illustrative example (adapted from Reckase, 2009) under the pretense that the item parameters are already known. Consider the likelihood surface and contour plots in Figure 7.1; our goal is to find the θ-coordinates that are most likely to produce the observed response, that is, the maximum of the likelihood surface. The topmost plots display the likelihood after person p answers the first item incorrectly (thus, so far the response pattern X_p only has one entry: 0). Based on the M2PL parameters of Item 1 ($a_1 = 1$, $a_2 = .5$, $c = 0$), the likelihood of responding incorrectly to this first item peaks in the lower left region of the contour plot. So, after a single incorrect response, our best guess is that person p is located somewhere along the lower end of both latent trait continua. Keep in mind, however, that "the lower end" could mean $\theta = \{-2, -2\}$, or it could mean $\theta = \{-10, 10\}$. At this point, person p has not given us enough information to make a more precise estimate.

The middle plots depict the likelihood after the respondent correctly answers a second item, which has parameters $a_1 = .5$, $a_2 = 1.5$, and $c = -1$. Now we know a bit more about person p's location. He is still likely to be located at the lower end of the θ_1 scale, but his current response pattern $X_p = \{01\}$ suggests he is located at the higher end of the θ_2 scale. Unfortunately, the peak of this likelihood is also undefined; the maximum is unbounded, so we still cannot obtain a precise estimate of person p's location.

The bottom plots display the likelihood after a correct response to Item 3, which has parameters $a_1 = 2$, $a_2 = .1$, and $c = .5$. The likelihood function now has a well-defined maximum, which is clearly indicated by the smallest circle in the contour plot. The peak suggests that $\theta \approx \{0, 1.5\}$ is the most likely combination of abilities to provide the response pattern $\mathbf{X}_p = \{011\}$ to the three items with parameters as defined earlier. As additional item responses are collected, the location will move around the θ-space, and the peak of the likelihood function will become more clearly defined.

This example might make it appear as though MIRT estimation is a simple extension of UIRT methods. As with other issues in MIRT, however, the presence of additional dimensions makes things far more statistically complicated. This chapter presents two fundamental challenges to MIRT estimation, followed by a general overview of various MIRT estimation methods and how they address these challenges. These methods will be described in fairly broad conceptual terms, following L. Cai and Thissen (2015); advanced technical details are provided in Baker and Kim (2004) and Fox (2010). Before we delve into MIRT estimation, however, it will be helpful to explicate two important, underappreciated estimation concepts that are intrinsic to the MML and EM approach: the missing data formulation and Fisher's Identity.

Missing Data Formulation

In our earlier review of UIRT estimation, we examined the likelihood of the model parameters given some response pattern. We referred to this function as the *observed* data likelihood. However, it would be most beneficial to determine the *complete* data likelihood, that is, the likelihood given the observed responses as well as any unobserved latent variables:

$$L\left(\gamma \mid \mathbf{X}, \theta\right) \propto \prod_{p=1}^{P} \prod_{i=1}^{I} \left[P_i\left(\theta; a_i, b_i\right)\right]^{x_{ip}} \left[1 - P_i\left(\theta; a_i, b_i\right)\right]^{1 - x_{ip}}. \tag{7.1}$$

The term on the left indicates that the likelihood of the item parameters γ is conditional on the complete data: the matrix $\mathbf{X}$ of all observed responses and the latent variable θ.[1] The motivation for this reformulation is this: If we could somehow observe the latent variable scores, then the complete

---

[1] Notice that Equation (7.1) does not include the prior distribution of person parameters $h(\theta)$ that we saw in the joint probability; this is because $h(\theta)$ does not depend on item parameters and, given θ, it becomes a constant.

Figure 7.1 The multidimensional likelihood function for response pattern $\mathbf{X}_p$ after incorrect response to item 1 ($a_1 = 1$, $a_2 = .5$, $c = 0$; top), correct response to Item 2 ($a_1 = .5$, $a_2 = 1.5$, $c = -1$; middle), and correct response to Item 3 ($a_1 = 2$, $a_2 = .1$, $c = .5$; bottom).

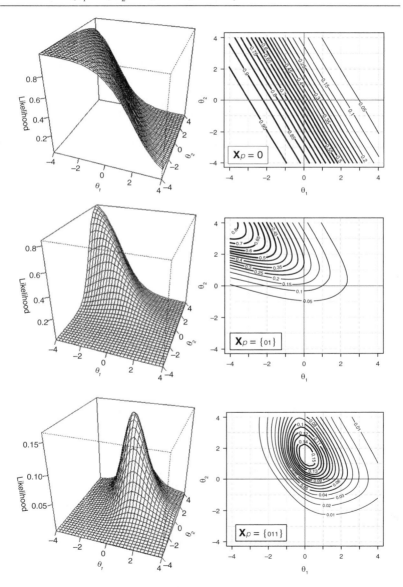

data likelihood would be found by simply multiplying the I item-specific likelihoods $\left[P_i\left(\bullet\right)^{x_{ip}} \right]\left[1 - P_i\left(\bullet\right)^{1-x_{ip}} \right]$. In that case, our UIRT model would be a multivariate logistic regression model and estimation would be fairly straightforward. Unfortunately, the typical conceptualization of latent variables tells us that such variables are, by their very definition, unobservable.

However, in a landmark paper, Dempster et al. (1977) supplied the key to dealing with the unobserved θ. Rather than thinking of latent variables as *unobservable*, Dempster and colleagues suggested that we could treat the latent variable scores as *missing* data. In the context of IRT, we can use this approach to think of the θ parameter in Equation (7.1) as missing data; the latent trait locations of each respondent can then be treated as missing at random, and statistical methods for handling missing data can be applied (see Little & Rubin, 2014, for the definitive overview of missing data analysis). The result of this reformulation is the complete data likelihood, which puts us in the manageable realm of multivariate logistic regression. To facilitate estimation even further, we will take the natural logarithm of Equation (7.1), which will allow us to work with sums rather than products. The result is the complete data log-likelihood for the item parameters:

$$
\begin{aligned}
\log L\left(\boldsymbol{\gamma} \mid \mathbf{X}, \theta\right) \propto &\sum\nolimits_{p=1}^{P} \sum\nolimits_{i=1}^{I} x_{ip} \log\left[P_i\left(\theta; a_i, b_i\right) \right] \\
&+ \sum\nolimits_{p=1}^{P} \sum\nolimits_{i=1}^{I} \left(1 - x_{ip}\right) \log\left[1 - P_i\left(\theta; a_i, b_i\right) \right]
\end{aligned}
\tag{7.2}
$$

A question remains, however: Although the missing data formulation allows us to obtain the complete data log-likelihood, thereby simplifying estimation, how can we be certain that the complete data parameter estimates are the same as the observed data parameter estimates? If we are to proceed with this approach, we need to ensure that the missing data formulation will yield the same parameter estimates as the original observed data formulation.

Fortunately, nearly a century ago, Fisher (1925) established the necessary link between the complete and observed data log-likelihoods. The statistical equality known as Fisher's Identity is given by

$$
\frac{\partial \log P\left(\mathbf{X}_p; \boldsymbol{\gamma}\right)}{\partial \boldsymbol{\gamma}} = \int \frac{\partial \log P\left(\mathbf{X}_p, \theta; \boldsymbol{\gamma}\right)}{\partial \boldsymbol{\gamma}} P\left(\theta \mid \mathbf{X}_p; \boldsymbol{\gamma}\right) d\theta.
\tag{7.3}
$$

The left side of this equation represents the gradient (i.e., the first derivative) of the *observed* data log-likelihood (presented back in Equation [2.10]). The right side of the equation includes two important terms. The first represents the gradient of the *complete* data log-likelihood (note the inclusion of the unobserved latent variable θ in the first term on the right side of the equation). The second represents the posterior distribution of the latent variable θ given the observed variables.

Putting it all together, Fisher's Identity in Equation (7.3) states that the gradient of the observed data log-likelihood is equivalent to the conditional expectation of the gradient of the complete data log-likelihood over the posterior distribution of θ. You will recall that the gradient is needed in order to locate the maximum of a likelihood function and thereby pinpoint the parameter estimates. Fisher's Identity holds that maximization of the conditional expected complete likelihood (which is an indirect but manageable task) will yield the parameter estimates that we would obtain if it were possible to maximize the observed likelihood (which is a direct but computationally unmanageable method).

Two Challenges

We will return to the missing data formulation and Fisher's Identity shortly, but for now, we can move on to MIRT estimation, which is beset by a pair of problems. The first problem we encounter relates to the complexity of the likelihood surface. In UIRT estimation, the likelihood function was a simple inverted parabola, and determining the maximum of this function was relatively trivial. In MIRT modeling, however, the likelihood function is a multidimensional surface that may have an extremely intricate topography, potentially full of valleys and peaks, and finding its maximum is usually a considerable computational challenge. Unfortunately, this surface does not belong to a named statistical family with known properties (e.g., the multivariate normal distribution) and must be mapped using advanced estimation techniques. This introduces our primary problem: If we want to obtain the parameter estimates, we need to find a way to compute the high-dimensional integral in the marginal probability of the likelihood function.

Through MML and the EM algorithm, as discussed in Chapter 2, we are able to determine the statistical parameter(s) of each item on a unidimensional test. To skirt the tricky integration in the marginal probability, Bock and Aitkin (1981) suggested the use of Gauss-Hermite quadrature (also known as numerical integration), a technique that has proved to be quite effective when dealing with unidimensional test instruments. However, the EM algorithm weakens in the face of high-dimensional integrals, as the increase in quadrature points quickly becomes computationally overwhelming. This introduces our second computational problem: As the number of dimensions in the model increases, the number of quadrature points grows exponentially. For example, the default UIRT settings in the mirt package include 61 quadrature points along a continuum from –6 to +6. If we add a second latent trait and want to keep the same degree of granularity in terms of quadrature, then we would need to evaluate the multivariate distributions across a grid of $61^2 = 3,721$ quadrature points. Adding a third latent trait in the model would require $61^3 = 226,981$ quadrature points. Clearly, quadrature-based MML quickly becomes intractable in the presence of multiple dimensions. This is known colloquially as the *curse of dimensionality,* and it severely restricts the usability of ordinary IRT estimation methods. In fact, Schilling and Bock (2005) noted that the EM algorithm has a practical limit of just two or three quadrature points per dimension when there are more than three dimensions. Consequently, much of the theoretical work in MIRT estimation has focused on alternative methods of approximating the marginal probability of the latent variables underlying the item responses. In the following, we briefly discuss three advances in this direction: adaptive quadrature, Bayesian estimation, and the Metropolis-Hastings Robbins-Monro MH-RM algorithm (see L.Cai, 2010a, for additional approaches and references for further reading).

Adaptive Quadrature

Schilling and Bock (2005) presented a compelling alternative to the integration problem: adaptive quadrature. In traditional (Gauss-Hermite) quadrature, the quadrature points are fixed at user-specified intervals across a reasonable range of θ. In the adaptive approach, as pioneered by Naylor and Smith (1982), the quadrature points are adjusted according to the shape of the posterior distribution. The reasoning is this: If the posterior indicates that the true parameter value is between, say, –1 and +1, then why should we be concerned with evaluating θ across a range that extends beyond these bounds? A more efficient approach would be to focus on the most likely range of θ, as suggested by the posterior distribution. Thus, we can refine and adjust our quadrature rules according to the mean μ and covariance matrix ψ of the posterior density.

The typical approach to identifying μ and ψ is to approximate (via further use of quadrature) the posterior means and covariance matrices at each iteration of the EM algorithm (Rabe-Hesketh, Skrondal, & Pickles, 2002;

Schilling & Bock, 2005). In the E-step, the quadrature points are based on the current shape of the posterior, as represented by moments μ and ψ. In the M-step, the maximum likelihood estimates of the parameters are obtained and updated approximations of μ and ψ are sent back to the E-step to begin the cycle anew. These iterations continue until the process converges on stable parameter estimates.

In a series of simulations, Schilling and Bock (2005) established the use of adaptive quadrature in IRT modeling and demonstrated its improved precision and efficiency relative to fixed quadrature estimation. By adjusting the EM iterations according to the shape of the posterior, the simulation results revealed that parameter estimates were more accurate, EM convergence was faster, and fewer quadrature points were required. Cagnone and Monari (2013) further demonstrated that the benefits of adaptive quadrature are especially pronounced when working with small sample sizes.

Although adaptive quadrature has become a popular tool in MIRT modeling, it does have limitations. The primary obstacle is still the curse of dimensionality; while the adaptive algorithm has proved to be more efficient and accurate than the fixed approach, it still has to cope with the exponential increase in quadrature points that comes with multidimensionality. Furthermore, as L. Cai (2008) demonstrated, adaptive quadrature-based EM does not automatically provide standard errors that are needed in order to quantify the accuracy of the parameter estimates.

Bayesian Estimation

A second alternative to fixed quadrature MML is found within the Bayesian framework of statistical inference. As noted by B. Muthén and Asparouhov (2012), Bayesian parameter estimates are analogous to the results that would be obtained had MML been a viable method. Two variations of Bayesian estimation have been utilized in approximating our problematic integral. The first adds a Bayesian twist to the EM algorithm by replacing the quadrature-based integration in the E-step with Monte Carlo (MC) integration (Wei & Tanner, 1990). More specifically, plausible values of the (missing) latent variables are imputed from the posterior predictive distribution of θ. This approach has been successfully applied in the analysis of item response data (e.g., Meng & Schilling, 1996) but suffers from convergence difficulties and other estimation inefficiencies (Jank, 2005).

The second variation is fully Bayesian estimation using Markov chain Monte Carlo (MCMC) methods. MCMC is a powerful tool for sampling from complex, high-dimensional probability distributions and, importantly for our purposes, computing expectations with respect to these distributions.

Thus, though we do not know the exact shape of the likelihood surface, MCMC can allow us to closely approximate it. A common strategy in defining this surface is to use a Gibbs sampler (Albert, 1992; Albert & Chib, 1993), in which parameter values are drawn from a series of marginal distributions conditional on the observed data and the other parameters in the model. MCMC has advantages over EM-based estimation because it does not involve numerical quadrature or computation of derivatives. However, Bayesian methods require careful specification of prior distributions, which can be quite complicated in MIRT modeling, and the MCMC process can be computationally burdensome. Interested readers can turn to Béguin and Glas (2001) or Martín-Fernández and Revuelta (2017) for advanced technical treatments of MCMC estimation in the context of MIRT modeling.

MH-RM Estimation

L. Cai (2010a) offered an alternate solution to the problems of MIRT estimation by combining the MH-RM algorithms. Although the statistics and reasoning behind this algorithm are beyond the scope of this volume, essentially, the MH-RM algorithm uses a Bayesian sampler to fill in the missing θ values, thereby facilitating ML estimation. The MH-RM algorithm follows three steps. First, starting values (i.e., initial parameter estimates) are supplied and many sets of missing θ values are imputed. These imputed values are drawn at random, using the MH sampler, from the posterior predictive distribution of the θ values given the observed item responses. Second, the matrix of imputed θ values is used to determine the complete data log-likelihood and its gradient and Hessian (i.e., first and second derivatives). L. Cai (2010a) invoked Fisher's Identity to prove that the Monte Carlo average of the complete data log-likelihood gradients will indicate the correct direction of ascent toward the maximum of the n-dimensional likelihood function. Thus, this second step will point us in the right direction; however, because the MH algorithm is a stochastic approximation method, the complete data imputations will be corrupted by sampling error. Consequently, in the third step, an RM filter is used to gradually filter out this noise as the parameters are recursively updated. The result is stable and precise estimation of the maximum of the complex multidimensional likelihood surface. In addition, this method improves on the alternatives by yielding the observed data information matrix, and thus the standard errors. However, readers should be aware that implementation of the MH-RM algorithm requires careful tuning (see L. Cai, 2010a). The MH-RM has been successfully employed in a number of comprehensive latent variable measurement modeling applications (e.g., Bashkov & DeMars, 2017; Chalmers, 2015; Chalmers & Flora, 2014; Monroe & Cai, 2014; Yang & Cai, 2014).

R Code

The adaptive quadrature approach can be implemented in R via the flirt package (Jeon, Rijmen, & Rabe-Hesketh, 2014). The fully Bayesian approach can be implemented in Stan software (Carpenter et al., 2017), which can be operated from within the R environment using the Rstan package (Stan Development Team, 2018). The MH-RM algorithm is built into the mirt package. The Companion Student Study Site includes R code that demonstrates how to estimate MIRT parameters within each approach.

Chapter 8

MIRT MODEL DIAGNOSTICS AND EVALUATION

An important component of any statistical modeling scenario is the diagnosis and evaluation of the model. A thorough statistical model appraisal can uncover its strengths and/or shortcomings, thereby identifying ways to improve the statistical rigor and usefulness of the model. IRT offers a number of evaluative and diagnostic techniques that can help us answer several important questions about the psychometric quality of a model. Is a MIRT model appropriate or necessary for the data that have been collected? If so, how can we select the correct model from among several competing models? Is each item response surface an accurate representation of the true probability of responding correctly? Does the multidimensionality in the overall model reflect the true structure of the item response data? This chapter aims to answer these and other questions by detailing several MIRT model diagnostics.

Dimensionality Assessment

A reasonable starting point in MIRT model evaluation is to ensure that a meaningful degree of multidimensionality is present in the data and that all dimensions are interpretable. In the context of item response data, J. Zhang and Stout (1999a) differentiate between two approaches to dimensionality assessment in IRT modeling. The first approach is more exploratory in nature and seeks to identify the degree to which the data depart from a unidimensional structure; the second, more confirmatory approach focuses on estimating the number of latent traits in the data and specifying their associations with each item. It should be noted that the most widely accepted methods of dimensionality assessment were developed in the context of continuous data analysis, including various factor analytic indicators of dimensionality such as eigenvalues/scree plots, parallel analysis, and principal components analysis. While these have some utility in categorical data analysis (e.g., de Ayala, 2009), we focus our attention instead on IRT-specific methods of dimensionality assessment.

In Chapter 2, we reviewed the data assumptions of UIRT models. The assumption of local independence holds that the data exhibit no dependencies beyond their association to the single latent trait underlying the item responses. In other words, the probability of correct response to one item should not depend on the probability of correct response to another item. Several statistical techniques for the detection of local independence violations include the Q_3 statistic (Yen, 1984), the model-based covariance (MBC) for item pairs (Reckase, 1997), and the LD-X^2 index (Chen & Thissen, 1997). Essentially, these indexes are based on the residual correlations among all item pairs, and a statistically significant correlation between the items in a given pair is evidence of local dependence. Both the Q_3 and LD-X^2 indexes are well established in the UIRT literature (e.g., Embretson & Reise, 2000; Thissen & Wainer, 2001) and will not be reviewed here, though the MBC is presented in the following. In general, it is important to note that the presence of local dependence does not necessarily mean that one of the items in the unruly pair must be deleted; instead, this local dependency could be intentionally specified in a MIRT model. For example, the assumption of local independence would be violated on the reading comprehension exam presented in Chapter 6, wherein several items pertain to a single passage; rather than removing any items, this cluster of related items could be represented as a testlet factor (Wainer, Bradlow, & Wang, 2007) in a MIRT model.

More recent research has focused on nonparametric approaches to dimensionality assessment, including the DIMTEST procedure (Stout, 1987) and the DETECT index (J. Zhang, 2007; J. Zhang & Stout, 1999b). Each of these indexes aims to quantify the degree of multidimensionality that is present in the matrix of item responses. Both DIMTEST and DETECT were developed according to the theory of "essential unidimensionality" (Stout, 1990); the core assumption of this theory is that the application of a UIRT model becomes less viable as the multidimensionality in the data increases. Thus, both approaches comb the data for the presence of any dimensions beyond the dominant latent trait underlying the response patterns (i.e., the common factor, for which the sum of raw item scores serves as a proxy).

The DETECT index has become fairly popular in IRT modeling. This index is based on the conditional covariances between pairs of items, that is, the statistical associations between pairs of items, conditional on the dominant dimension. To borrow a factor analytic term, the DETECT index is largest when the response data follow a *simple structure* (Thurstone, 1947), meaning there are no cross-loadings among the subdimensions: Each item is associated with, at most, one and only one subdimension beyond the dominant dimension. If simple structure can be assumed, then items that measure the same subdimension will exhibit positive conditional covariances, while items that measure different subdimensions will exhibit negative conditional covariances (Mroch & Bolt, 2006).

The DETECT index can be represented as

$$D(P) = \frac{1}{n(n-1)/2} \sum_{i<j} (-1)^{C_{ij}} (C\hat{C}ov_{ij} - \overline{C\hat{C}ov}), \qquad (8.1)$$

where P represents a particular partitioning of the items into clusters, n is the number of items, $CCov_{ij}$ is the conditional covariance between items i and j, and $\hat{CCov}$ is the mean conditional covariance among all item pairs. The indicator function $C_{ij} = 0$ if items i and j belong to the same cluster c, or 1 if the items belong to different clusters. When the data are perfectly unidimensional, meaning there are no secondary subdimensions, then each item pair will have an expected conditional covariance of 0. When even a slight degree of multidimensionality is present, then the conditional covariance will deviate from zero. In practice, a statistical algorithm is used to identify the item clustering that maximizes the DETECT index. More specifically, if the data follow approximate simple structure, then the algorithm will maximize Equation (8.1) at cluster partition P of the scale, where each cluster represents a different homogeneous dimension.

According to J. Zhang and Stout (1999b), the maximum DETECT value "indicates the amount of multidimensionality the test displays, that is, the size of the departure from being perfectly fitting to a unidimensional model" (p. 219). Low DETECT values indicate essential unidimensionality: The data may not be perfectly unidimensional, but the degree of multidimensionality is ignorable. Higher DETECT values indicate a departure from unidimensionality, thereby suggesting that a MIRT model (or other multidimensional measurement model) might be needed (Roussos & Ozbek, 2006; Stout et al., 1996). In the original development of the DETECT index, Stout et al. (1996) suggested that $D(P) \leq 0.1$ reflects that the data are essentially unidimensional while $D(P) \leq 1.0$ indicates the presence of "sizable dimensionality" (p. 348). Roussos and Ozbek (2006) constructed a more precise yardstick for the DETECT index, with proposed hatch marks for essential unidimensionality/weak multidimensionality ($D(P) \leq 0.2$), weak to moderate multidimensionality ($0.2 < D(P) \leq 0.4$, moderate to large multidimensionality ($0.4 < D(P) \leq 1.0$), and strong multidimensionality ($D(P) > 1.0$). Interested readers should consult the Companion Student Study Site for R code that demonstrates how to implement the DETECT algorithm using the sirt package.

Finally, it should be noted that the bifactor model, which we previously discussed in the context of the two-tier model, can also be used to assess unidimensionality (Reise, Morizot, & Hays, 2007; Stucky & Edelen, 2015). More specifically, the bifactor model can be used to determine whether the item response data, which always includes some degree of multidimensionality, can be considered "unidimensional enough" for accurate UIRT modeling. Basically, if the general factor accounts for a substantial proportion of the common variance among the items, then the specific factors can be treated as ignorable nuisance factors; in such a case, it would then be appropriate to apply a unidimensional model. If the specific factors play a larger role in explaining the common variance, then a MIRT or other multidimensional measurement model may be suitable.

We turn now to assessing the structure of data that are not expected to be unidimensional. Rather than detecting departures from unidimensionality, one may instead be concerned with modeling the multidimensionality that is hypothesized to exist in the data (e.g., due to testlets or other item content clusters that have been built into the test design). Typical approaches are exploratory in nature: The user specifies multiple models (e.g., a 2-dimensional model vs. a 3-dimensional model) and then compares the model via goodness-of-fit statistics or other model comparison methods (both of which are described later). The multidimensional structure that best represents the data is usually selected as the "correct" solution.

There are also confirmatory methods of establishing the multidimensionality in item response data. One promising development in this direction is the generalized dimensionality discrepancy measure (GDDM; Levy & Svetina, 2011). The GDDM is based on the model-based covariance (MBC) for item pairs (Reckase, 1997):

$$MBC_{ii'} = \frac{1}{N}\sum_{p=1}^{N}\left[x_{ip} - E\left(x_{ip} \mid \theta_{p}, \gamma_{i}\right)\right]\left[x_{i'p} - E\left(x_{i'p} \mid \theta_{p}, \gamma_{i'}\right)\right], \qquad (8.2)$$

where N is the number of respondents; $E\left(x_{ip} \mid \theta_{p}, \gamma_{i}\right)$ is the expectation of the response x of person p to item i, given the person parameters in θ_{p} and the item parameters in γ_{i}; and the subscript ii' represents an item pair. The MBC is a local dependence measure that, like the DETECT index, estimates the conditional covariances within each item pair.

The GDDM proposed by Levy and Svetina (2011) is the mean of the absolute values of MBC across all unique item pairs:

$$GDDM = \frac{\sum_{i \neq i'}\left|MBC_{ii'}\right|}{I(I-1)}, \qquad (8.3)$$

where I is the number of items on the test. In simple terms, the GDDM represents the average amount of local dependence among all item pairs. This approach is essentially a multidimensional extension of the maximum DETECT index described earlier: While the DETECT index conditions on a single dominant dimension, the GDDM conditions on (potentially) multiple dimensions. Interested readers should consult Levy and Svetina (2011), whose simulation and empirical studies provide evidence of the utility of GDDM in confirming a hypothesized multidimensional structure.

In fact, their work has demonstrated that the GDDM can be successfully applied with dichotomous models (including the 3PL model), polytomous models, and continuous data without any restriction on approximate simple structure or complete data (Svetina & Levy, 2012).

Test-Level Fit Assessment

Suppose we have used one of the methods above to verify that our data are multidimensional and have proceeded to fit an appropriate MIRT model to these data. The next step is to investigate whether the chosen model closely represents the observed data. When data are continuous, the available modeling methods (e.g., factor analysis, structural equation modeling) provide an abundance of statistics and indexes for assessing overall goodness-of-fit. As we will see, this is certainly not the case when modeling categorical item response data. Before we delve any deeper into this topic, it would be beneficial to review a few of the rudiments of categorical data analysis.

Discrete item response data can be arranged in an m-dimensional contingency table of the observed response pattern proportions. Table 8.1 presents a simple case: two dichotomous items. The columns and rows represent correct and incorrect responses to Items 1 and 2, respectively, and the cells contain the observed proportions of each possible two-item response pattern. The upper left cell of the table, for example, reflects the proportion of respondents in the sample who produced pattern 00, meaning they failed to correctly answer either item.

In this context, we can conceptualize goodness-of-fit as the discrepancy between the observed proportions and the model-implied, or expected, probabilities of each response pattern. If the observed values in the cells are

Table 8.1 A 2 × 2 contingency table of observed correct response proportions.

		Item 1		
		0	1	
Item 2	0	π_{00}	π_{10}	$\pi_{.0}$
	1	π_{01}	π_{11}	$\pi_{.1}$
		$\pi_{0.}$	$\pi_{1.}$	

close to what the model tells us we should expect them to be, then we have good model–data fit. Specifically, this contingency table could be analyzed using Pearson's chi-square statistic:

$$X^2 = N \sum_c \frac{\left(p_c - \hat{\pi}_c\right)^2}{\hat{\pi}_c}, \tag{8.4}$$

where N is the sample size, P_c is the observed proportion in cell c, and $\hat{\pi}_c$ is the expected probability in cell c. The expected values are based on the *marginal* proportions (i.e., the row and column totals along the margins of the contingency table): $\hat{\pi}_c = \left[\left(p_{row}\right)\left(p_{col}\right)\right] / N$.

A fundamental issue in analyzing contingency table data is that, by definition, $\pi_{00} + \pi_{10} + \pi_{01} + \pi_{11}$ must sum to 1. For example, suppose that 100 individuals responded to our dichotomous two-item measure; 10 incorrectly answered both items, 40 correctly answered Item 1 only, and 30 correctly answered Item 2 only. Because these frequencies (and the corresponding proportions) must sum to 1, we can fill in the missing information (10 + 40 + 30 + __ = 100) to determine that 20 individuals (or a proportion of 0.20) correctly answered both items.

The fact that the proportions must sum to 1 introduces a problem: As the number of items (and/or the number of response categories) in the contingency table increases, the proportions quickly become quite small. Thus, as the number of possible response patterns increases, the expected frequencies become quite small and standard p-values cannot be used (Bartholomew & Tzamourani, 1999). This is known as the *sparse contingency table problem*. With two dichotomous items, there are only $2^2 = 4$ possible response patterns, so it is trivial to secure a sample size large enough to provide the required frequencies in each cell. However, the number of cells in a contingency table increases as an exponential function of test length: A relatively brief instrument with just 10 dichotomous items includes $2^{10} = 1,024$ possible response patterns, while a dichotomous 20-item measure includes well over 1 million possible patterns. Maydeu-Olivares (2013) placed practical limits on the number of items and response categories, noting that the classical chi-square p-value becomes inaccurate when a test is composed of more than five items that include four or more response categories. Clearly, we need a workaround to the sparse contingency table problem.

As we established earlier, Table 8.1 can be described using the probabilities of all four response patterns $\pi = (\pi_{00}, \pi_{10}, \pi_{01}, \pi_{11})$. This is precisely how the Pearson X^2 assesses goodness of fit, which is why it can be considered a full-information fit statistic. But we could also ignore the all-incorrect [00] response pattern and focus only on the *univariate* probabilities of correct response $\boldsymbol{\pi}_1 = (\pi_{1\cdot}, \pi_{\cdot1})$, meaning the marginal probabilities of correct response to Item $(\pi_{1\cdot})$ and to Item $2(\pi_{\cdot1})$, and the *bivariate* probability of responding correctly to both items $\boldsymbol{\pi}_2 = (\pi_{11})$. Both descriptions would be identical, but the latter uses less information in characterizing the probabilities in the table.

Thus, as a remedy to the sparse contingency table problem, so-called limited-information fit statistics have been introduced to IRT modeling. Rather than dealing with the complete information (i.e., all cells in the contingency table), limited-information fit statistics are based on pooling the cell entries. More specifically, the univariate and bivariate proportions of correct response/endorsement (i.e., the lower-order margins of the contingency table) are used to pool cells for goodness-of-fit assessment.

Examples of limited-information fit statistics that have been applied in MIRT modeling include the Y_2 (L. Cai, Maydeu-Olivares, Coffman, & Thissen, 2006) and R_2 (Reiser, 1996) indexes, as well as the *Mr* family of statistics (Maydeu-Olivares & Joe, 2005). We focus only on the latter, as it has received far more attention in the MIRT modeling literature. One particular member of the *Mr* family is the M_2 limited-information fit statistic, which has recently become quite popular in MIRT model evaluation. This statistic is formulated as

$$M_2 = N\hat{\mathbf{e}}_2'\hat{\mathbf{C}}_2\hat{\mathbf{e}}_2, \tag{8.5}$$

where N is the number of respondents, $\hat{\mathbf{e}}_2$ is the vector of univariate and bivariate residual proportions, and $\hat{\mathbf{C}}_2$ is a complex weight matrix. The statistical details behind M_2 are too involved to present in this volume, though interested readers can explore the *Mr* family of fit statistics in Maydeu-Olivares and Joe (2005, 2006) as well as a comprehensive overview of limited-information fit assessment in Maydeu-Olivares (2013).

For our purposes, there are three important aspects of the M_2 statistic. First, this limited-information fit statistic circumvents the sparse contingency table problem by utilizing only the first- and second-order moments. Second, the M_2 value can be evaluated against a χ^2 distribution to obtain a *p*-value that indicates the degree of perfect fit. Third, because perfect fit is unlikely to be observed in empirical data, Maydeu-Olivares and Joe (2014) proposed RMSEA$_2$, an index of adequate fit based on the M_2 statistic:

$$\text{RMSEA}_2 = \sqrt{\frac{M_2 - df}{N \times df}}, \tag{8.6}$$

where df represents the degrees of freedom for M_2. Adequate model fit is indicated by $RMSEA_2 \leq .05 / (K - 1)$, where K is the number of response categories (Maydeu-Olivares & Joe, 2014). Overall, while the evaluation of test-level goodness of fit presents a number of challenges, the M_2 statistic appears to have considerable utility in MIRT modeling. Fit assessment is an open area of research, and recent years have seen the $M2$ extended to ordinal data (L. Cai & Hansen, 2013) and applied in the context of diagnostic classification modeling (Hansen, Cai, Monroe, & Li, 2016). Maydeu-Olivares (2013) comments, however, that more work is needed in the area of IRT fit assessment, particularly with regard to the performance of M_2 and other fit statistics in applied settings rather than simulation studies. See the Companion Student Study Site for R code related to overall goodness-of-fit assessment using the mirt package.

Item-Level Fit Assessment

After evaluating the test-level goodness of fit of the model, we can proceed to an item-level fit analysis. If the fit of the overall model is poor, then an item fit analysis might help to uncover the sources of misfit. Even if the overall fit seems adequate, an item fit analysis should be carried out, as it may improve the model with regard to interpretation, usefulness, and other important psychometric qualities.

Item fit analysis involves comparing the model predictions with the actual response patterns. In UIRT, item fit can be evaluated by computing the S-X^2 statistic (Orlando & Thissen, 2000, 2003) for each item. Essentially, this item fit statistic compares the observed and expected proportions of correct and incorrect responses for each total score k in the sample. For example, suppose that 1,000 students completed a 50-point exam, and 20 of the students earned the same score of $k = 45$. Suppose we find that, among those 20 students, 16 were able to answer Item 1 correctly; this would indicate a correct response proportion of 0.8 among the students who performed well on the overall exam. We could repeat the process for every total score $k = 0, 1, 2, \ldots, 50$, thereby obtaining the observed proportions of correct response across the full range of possible test scores. We would anticipate finding that the correct response proportion for Item 1 is lower when the total score is lower and higher when the total score is higher. In fact, we would hope to find that a plot of these proportions would follow a logistic function. The expected proportions are those predicted by our IRT model; if the observed and expected proportions are similar, then we conclude that the item fits well. The S-X^2 statistic is given by

$$\text{S-X}^2 = \sum_{k=1}^{K} N_k \frac{\left(O_{ik} - E_{ik}\right)^2}{E_{ik}\left(1 - E_{ik}\right)}, \tag{8.7}$$

where N_k is the number of observations of score category k; O_{ik} is the observed proportion of correct responses to item i for score k, which is simply counted from the item response contingency table; and E_{ik} is the expected proportion of correct response. The sampling distribution of the S-X^2 statistic approximates a χ^2 distribution with degrees of freedom equal to K (the total number of score categories) minus the number of modeled item parameters (Orlando & Thissen, 2000).

To understand how item fit evaluation works in the presence of multidimensionality, we can begin with a visualization. Figure 8.1 depicts a familiar M2PL response surface, though we now see a cloud of points (or spheres, as we are dealing with a 3-dimensional space) above and below the surface. The white spheres above the surface represent observed correct response proportions that are underestimated by the model (i.e., $E_{ik} < O_{ik}$),

Figure 8.1   Observed response proportions and model expectations in a multidimensional space.

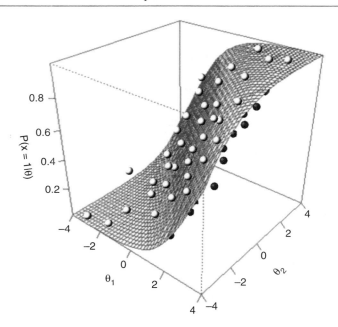

while the black spheres below the surface represent observed proportions that are overestimated by the model (i.e., $E_{ik} > O_{ik}$). The spheres vary in their residual distance from the surface; when fitting a MIRT model, we hope to see that the response surface comes as close as possible to the observed data. If this occurs, then the residuals will be negligible and the $S - X^2$ analysis will not flag any items for significant misfit.

Fortunately, MIRT item fit can be evaluated by direct application of Equation (8.7) (B. Zhang & Stone, 2008). N_k and O_{ik} are determined just as before, but to compute E_{ik} the expected proportion of correct response, we need to revisit the multidimensional likelihood function. For relative simplification, we will extend UIRT likelihood in Equation (2.9) to the 2-dimensional M2PL model, which gives us the likelihood of a particular dichotomous response pattern X given the respondent's location along latent traits θ_1 and θ_2:

$$L(\mathbf{X} \mid \theta_1, \theta_2) = \prod_{i=1}^{I} \left[P_i\left(\theta_1, \theta_2\right) \right]^{x_i} \left[1 - P_i\left(\theta_1, \theta_2\right) \right]^{1-x_i}. \qquad (8.8)$$

Here, $P_i(\theta_1, \theta_2)$ represents the height of the M2PL item response surface at coordinates θ_1 and θ_2, while x_i is the observed response of 0 or 1.

The first step in computing the S-X^2 statistic is to add up the likelihoods of each total score k:

$$S_k = \sum L(\mathbf{X} \mid \theta_1, \theta_2). \qquad (8.9)$$

Consider, for example, a three-item test that is scored dichotomously, yielding $2^3 = 8$ possible response patterns: 000, 001, 010, 011, 100, 101, 110, and 111. If we sum within each pattern, we obtain total scores of $k = 0, 1, 1, 2, 1, 2, 2,$ and 3, respectively. Equation (8.9) says that the joint likelihood of each total score k is found by summing the likelihoods of all response patterns that sum to k. The likelihood of a total score of 0 (all items answered incorrectly) is simply the likelihood of pattern 000, and the likelihood of a total score of 3 (all items answered correctly) is the likelihood of pattern 111. However, there are multiple patterns that sum to 1 and 2. The joint likelihood of a total score of 1 is therefore the sum of the likelihoods for all patterns that sum to 1 (i.e., patterns 001, 010, and 100). Similarly, the joint likelihood of a total score of 2 is the sum of the likelihoods of patterns 011, 101, and 110.

Once S_k has been determined for item i, we can then compute the expected correct response proportion (i.e., based on our MIRT model):

$$E_{ik} = \frac{\iint P_i\left(\theta_1, \theta_2\right) S_{k-1}^{*i} h\left(\theta_1, \theta_2\right) \partial\theta_1 \partial\theta_2}{\iint S_k h\left(\theta_1, \theta_2\right) \partial\theta_1 \partial\theta_2}, \qquad (8.10)$$

where $h\left(\theta_1, \theta_2\right)$ is the prior population distribution of the latent traits (typically assumed to be bivariate normal unless otherwise specified), and S_{k-1}^{*i} is the likelihood for total score $k-1$ without item i (i.e., the "rest score"). Fortunately, the thorny integration in Equation (7.3) can be easily approximated using standard Gauss-Hermite quadrature, as described earlier. Note that item fit can be evaluated using the mirt package in R; example code is provided in the Companion Student Study Site.

Model Comparison Methods

The model evaluation methods discussed thus far are typically used to inspect various aspects of a single model. It is not uncommon, however, for a researcher to consider multiple representations of the same data set. In such a case, several methods of model comparison can be used to evaluate a model in relative (rather than absolute) terms. For example, competing hypotheses may lead a researcher to fit a bifactor model and a testlet response model to the same data. There are several types of statistical evidence that can be used to provide support for one of these models relative to the other. We will briefly discuss the likelihood ratio test, information-theoretic indexes, and Bayes factors.

The likelihood ratio (LR) test can be used when comparing models that are nested, which means one of the models can be specified by constraining certain parameters in the other model (revisit our earlier survey of the two-tier IFA model for examples of nesting). The LR test statistic, ΔG^2, is the difference between the deviances of the two models, where deviance is defined as $-2\log(MLE)$ and MLE is the maximum likelihood estimate. ΔG^2 is approximately χ^2-distributed with degrees of freedom equal to the difference in the number of free parameters in each model. We can therefore estimate the statistical significance of ΔG^2 such that the model with the significantly smaller deviance is the better representation of the item response data (Baker & Kim, 2004). It is important to note, however, that ΔG^2 is highly sensitive to model misspecification and requires a large sample (see Maydeu-Olivares & Cai, 2006).

A second approach allows for comparisons among models that are not nested. This introduces a slight problem, however. In statistical modeling, increased parametric complexity (i.e., a greater number of freely estimated parameters) will improve goodness of fit; if we want to make an accurate comparison between models, then we will need to include some sort of adjustment for this unfair advantage. The Akaike information criterion (AIC; Akaike, 1974) and the Bayesian information criterion (BIC; Schwarz, 1978) are popular relative fit indexes that both follow the general form of "criterion = goodness-of-fit + penalty for complexity." Specifically, $AIC = -2\log(MLE) + 2k$ and $BIC = -2\log(MLE) + k\log(N)$, where k is the number of estimated parameters in the model and N is the sample size. As indexes, and not test statistics, AIC and BIC do not permit significance tests. However, they do allow for relative comparison among competing models such that the model with the lowest AIC and/or BIC is deemed to better represent the data.

AIC, BIC, and the LR test are based on maximum likelihood estimation of the model parameters and are not suitable when Bayesian estimation has been used (Lin & Dayton, 1997). In the context of MCMC estimation, models can be compared via the deviance information criterion (DIC; Spiegelhalter, Best, Carlin, & van der Linde, 2002). Like the AIC and BIC, this index assesses goodness of fit and includes a penalty for complexity, but DIC differs by employing a Bayesian (rather than likelihood-based) measure of fit known as the posterior mean deviance. As with other information criteria, the better model is the one with the lower DIC.

Finally, an alternate Bayesian approach is to compare two models via computation of a Bayes factor (BF; Gelfand, 1996). In the context of MIRT, the BF is the ratio of the marginal likelihoods of the observed data in each of the two models. A BF > 1 indicates that the model in the numerator of the ratio is a better representation of the data, while a BF < 1 indicates that the model in the denominator is preferred. Further details regarding the BF in the context of MIRT modeling are provided by Bolt and Lall (2003). Various relative fit indexes, including AIC, BIC, and DIC, can be extracted from a MIRT model using the mirt package in R; see the Companion Student Study Site for example code.

Chapter 9

MIRT APPLICATIONS

MIRT is a thriving area of methodological research—quantitative researchers and statisticians are continually developing new multidimensional models, model evaluation techniques, estimation methods, and other technical innovations. In this final chapter, we focus instead on a handful of the many novel, creative, and interesting MIRT applications that have been developed in recent years. Several of the MIRT applications that follow (e.g., linking and equating, differential item functioning, computerized adaptive testing) are extensions of well-established UIRT methods, while others (e.g., longitudinal MIRT, multilevel MIRT) have arisen as a direct result of the statistical advantages and sophistication of MIRT modeling.

Linking and Equating

Suppose we have two students, Tyrone and Martha, and we wish to compare their geographic knowledge. Unfortunately, these two students have responded to different forms of a geography exam. Both forms consist of questions about land masses, national capitals, bodies of water, and the like, but each form includes several unique items that do not appear on the other form. To make it more specific, let's say both forms include the same six questions, but Tyrone's form included four unique questions, while Martha's form included five unique questions. That is, although both forms were intended to measure geographic comprehension, Tyrone and Martha responded to test forms that differed in terms of length and content. Suppose both students answered eight items correctly, meaning Tyrone correctly answered $8/10 = 80\%$ of his items while Martha correctly answered $8/11 = 72.7\%$ of her items. Can these scores be compared directly? Would it be accurate to conclude that Tyrone truly possesses a higher level of geography knowledge than Martha?

In classical test theory, comparing scores from different tests requires that the tests are parallel, meaning they exhibit equal means and variances, as well as equal covariances with external variables (Gulliksen, 1950). However, even in the simplest case—two alternate test forms that have been purposefully designed to be parallel—violations of strict parallelism may abound: The items on one form may be more or less difficult or discriminating than the other, there may be unintended dissimilarities with regard to reliability or other psychometric properties, or perhaps most problematically, differences in test form content may result in the measurement of different constructs. Clearly, the classical requirement of parallelism is impractical and severely limits our ability to make accurate comparisons between scores from different tests. Fortunately, IRT enables us to relax this constraint.

A long-recognized benefit of IRT over classical test theory is the ability to equate the scores of alternate tests. *Linking* and *equating* are the IRT processes used to ensure that the θ estimates from different tests or separate calibrations can be placed on the same scale and thereby meaningfully compared. For the scores of different tests to be truly equated, five conditions must be satisfied (Dorans & Holland, 2000): The tests must measure the same construct, they must be equally reliable, they must yield identical expected scores, the equating function must be symmetrical (i.e., the transformation of Tyrone's test to Martha's should be the inverse of the transformation of Martha's test to Tyrone's), and the equating function must hold across all subpopulations. Although these criteria are unlikely to be perfectly met in most real data analyses, IRT methods can help us to (reasonably) satisfy each of these requirements.

In UIRT, the equating process involves the computation of linking coefficients that effectively shift and stretch either the item response functions (Haebara, 1980) or the overall test characteristic curve (Stocking & Lord, 1983) of the focal test to bring it into alignment with the reference test. By equating the θ scores, we minimize any differences between the tests (e.g., difficulty, reliability, etc.), and scores from alternate tests are then *interchangeable*: They have been equated and can now be directly compared. This interchangeability is possible because IRT measures respondents' true abilities, which are assumed to be stable; consistent; and, most important, independent of the actual items being administered.

MIRT linking is conceptually identical to UIRT linking: We will apply the same shift-and-stretch technique to align our items/tests, though the UIRT methods described earlier will, of course, need to be extended to the multidimensional parameter space. Technically, MIRT linking involves what is known as a Procrustean transformation (Mulaik, 1972), wherein a matrix of item properties (or the estimated θ distribution) is transformed to bring it into alignment with a reference matrix. This transformation involves complex matrix algebra that is beyond the scope of this discussion, so we will briefly focus instead on a visualization of the MIRT linking process.

Let us return to our 2-dimensional latent trait plane (denoted by dimensions θ_1 and θ_2) from earlier chapters. Our goal is to estimate the set of linking coefficients that will allow us to alter the latent trait plane of an alternate test (denoted by dimensions θ_1^* and θ_2^*) so that it can be

Figure 9.1 Illustration of the procrustean transformations involved in MIRT linking.

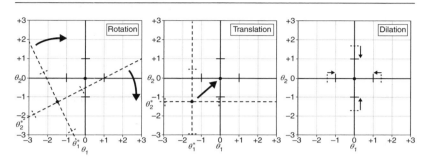

superimposed on the reference test. This may involve one or more of the following transformations (as illustrated in Figure 9.1): rotation, translation, and/or dilation. Rotation involves revolving the θ_1^* and θ_2^* axes so that they are parallel to the referent θ_1 and θ_2 axes; translation involves relocating the axes of the focal group so that they are overlaid on the referent axes; and dilation involves shrinking or expanding the axes (usually by adjusting the standard deviations) so that each set of axes adheres to the same scale.

The mathematical details of these transformations are beyond our present discussion, though interested readers should consult Weeks (2015) for a thorough yet accessible overview to MIRT linking, including the equation set that will yield the necessary linking coefficients and a comprehensive empirical application. Moreover, Weeks demonstrates how MIRT linking techniques are able to address each of the equating criteria outlined by Dorans and Holland (2000), as presented earlier. He also presents a thorough and informative application of multidimensional linking using data from math assessment that was administered across multiple years.

R Code

Multidimensional (and unidimensional) linking and equating can be conducted in R using the plink package (Weeks, 2015).

Differential Item Functioning

Differential item functioning (DIF) is present when the probability of a correct response is significantly different for respondents who belong to different groups but have similar levels of the latent trait. In line with this definition, standard UIRT methods for DIF detection typically involve statistical comparisons between the item response functions of two groups, known as the referent and focal groups. If the item response functions are not identical, then referent and focal group respondents who are located at the same point along the θ scale will have unequal probabilities of responding correctly (or, in the polytomous case, endorsing the same response option).

In the UIRT case, the presence of DIF between groups indicates that the response probability is affected by some unintended influence: a so-called nuisance dimension (beyond the "target trait," or the primary trait of interest) that alters the response probability in one of the groups. As Lord (1980) noted, "if many of the items are found to be seriously biased, it appears that the items are not strictly unidimensional" (p. 220). In that sense, we can conceptualize DIF in UIRT modeling as a result of unintentional multidimensionality in the data. However, a unidimensional model, by definition, cannot explicitly account for these nuisance dimensions; group differences may be detected, but it will be difficult to confidently identify the cause(s) of the DIF. Conducting such a DIF analysis would be conceptually similar to identifying local dependence violations among testlets and proceeding with a unidimensional model anyway. And just as a multidimensional item factor structure (such as the testlet response model) can be used to model and interpret local dependencies, a multidimensional approach to DIF analysis can be used to model and interpret between-group differences in response probabilities.

Accordingly, psychometric researchers have suggested a number of ways to utilize this multidimensional perspective in detecting DIF. These include nonparametric methods such as the Mantel-Haenszel test (Holland & Thayer, 1988) and the simultaneous item bias procedure (SIBTEST; Shealy & Stout, 1993), as well as latent variable modeling approaches (e.g., specifying the secondary dimensions in a testlet response model [Wang, Bradlow, Wainer, & Muller, 2008], as discussed in Chapter 6).

A more complicated matter, however, is the detection of DIF in tests that are intentionally multidimensional: tests that have been designed to measure multiple target dimensions. In this case, adverse influences on the response probability must be detected beyond the multiple target traits that have been purposefully built into the model. That is, the target traits in the model and the potentially DIF-causing nuisance dimensions must be isolated and addressed separately. This issue is the focus of ongoing research. One promising approach is to employ a bifactor MIRT model; Fukuhara and Kamata (2011) demonstrated how the bifactor structure can be used to detect DIF on a multidimensional (testlet-based) test instrument. More recent suggestions for handling DIF in MIRT contexts include multidimensional extensions of the likelihood ratio test and an adaptation of the multiple indicators multiple causes model (see Lee, Bulut, & Suh, 2017).

Examples of multidimensional DIF applications are given by Fletcher and Hattie (2005) with regard to gender differences in physical self-descriptions, and Walker, Zhang, and Surber (2008) in evaluating differences in mathematics performance among students with varying reading proficiencies. In both of these studies, the researchers used the methods described above to uncover problematic levels of DIF on multidimensional test items. Importantly, both papers discuss the implications of multidimensional DIF and offer suggestions on how it should be addressed in real-world scenarios.

R Code

Multidimensional DIF analysis can be conducted in R using the mirt package (Chalmers, 2012) by utilizing the DIF() command after running a multiple-groups MIRT analysis.

Computerized Adaptive Testing

Another benefit of IRT is that it provides a framework for computerized adaptive testing (CAT). CAT is a testing procedure in which the item administration adapts to the ability of the examinee. For instance, if you respond correctly to a moderately difficult item, then the CAT procedure will follow up with a more difficult item; if you respond incorrectly, then you will be given an easier item. CAT usually proceeds by first estimating the location of the respondent along the θ scale, then selecting the item (from an IRT-calibrated item bank) that best measures a higher (or lower) location, administering the item, collecting and scoring the response, and then updating the location estimate accordingly. This process is repeated until some stopping criterion has been met (e.g., when the standard error dips below some prespecified threshold). This is, of course, an oversimplification of CAT; indeed, entire textbooks have been written on the subject (e.g., van der Linden & Glas, 2000; Wainer, Dorans, Flaugher, Green, & Mislevy, 2000). However, this concise description opens the door for a brief discussion of the application of CAT in MIRT modeling.

Unsurprisingly, multidimensionality introduces several complications to the CAT process. One problem relates to the estimation of the respondent's location. In UIRT, this is a relatively trivial matter because the respondent will be located somewhere along the latent trait scale; in MIRT, the respondent will be located somewhere within the latent trait space. Thus, estimation would need to be carried out using one of the MIRT estimation algorithms described in Chapter 7.

The more complex issue relates to item selection. It would be inefficient to administer an item that is too difficult, or too easy, because it will not provide much information about the true location of the respondent. In UIRT, items are selected based on criteria specified by the researcher. A common technique is to select the most informative item that has a difficulty parameter just above (or below) the respondent's current θ estimate. For example, if the respondent's current ability estimate is $\theta = 1$ and the previous item was answered correctly, then the next item might be the most informative item in the difficulty range of, say, 1.25 to 1.50.

Of course, when there are multiple dimensions, item selection is not so straightforward. If we want to administer the most informative item, we need to consider that the amount of information changes depending on the direction of measurement. Suppose that after 10 items have been administered, our current estimate of the respondent's location in the latent space is $\theta = \{1,1\}$. If we compute the test information (where the "test" is the 10 items that have already been answered) in all directions from the θ-point, we will find a greater accumulation of information in certain regions of the latent space and less accumulation in others. Ideally, we want information to accumulate across a sizable region of the latent space; this would indicate that the test provides precise measurement at every θ-point.

With regard to item selection in MIRT CAT, the most useful item to administer next would be located in the area of the latent space that has the lowest accumulation of overall test information. Thus, we can compute the information in every direction from the current θ-point, travel toward the region that has accumulated the least information, and then select the most informative item in that region. While this may seem counterintuitive, this tactic will identify the item that best contributes to the overall measurement precision of the adaptive test. Note that this is just one of several approaches to the challenging task of item selection in MIRT CAT; see Chapter 10 of Reckase (2009) for details regarding additional item selection procedures.

CAT has long been a popular area of research, and thanks to advances in computing power and software, it is now relatively easy for practitioners to design and administer multidimensional CAT programs. Consequently, many recent applications and empirical examples can be found in the educational, psychological, and methodological literature. Informative applications of multidimensional CAT include the clinical work of Morris, Bass, Lee, and Neapolitan (2017) in measuring patient-report emotional distress, and Y. Zheng, Chang, and Chang (2013) in their bifactor CAT for assessing general health status along with specific physical and mental well-being.

R Code

Multidimensional adaptive tests can be designed and optimized in R using the mirtCAT package (Chalmers, 2015). This package allows users to not only create a CAT but also to generate an HTML interface for computerized administration and data collection.

Applications of the Two-Tier Item Factor Structure

In Chapter 6, the two-tier item factor analysis model was presented as a flexible structure for handling complex item response data. Because of this flexibility, the two-tier model can be applied in a wide range of research contexts. The most readily apparent use of this model is in handling complex educational assessment data. Large-scale assessments (e.g., the Programme for International Student Assessment, the NAEP) often use testlets to measure broad topics like reading, mathematics, and science. In Chapter 6, we discussed testlets in the context of reading literacy, but this testing format is also common in math and science, where a cluster of items may refer to a graph, table, or figure. The testlet structure within each broad topic suggests that the reading, math, and science assessment data could be modeled using three separate bifactor structures.

Consider, however, the relationships among these constructs. They are all likely to be correlated with one another: Science items may require both numerical literacy and reading proficiency, and many math problems must be read before they can be solved. Thus, it may be beneficial to account for these correlations rather than fitting separate models. Fortunately, the two-tier structure allows one to model correlated broad dimensions (in the primary tier) and specific factors (in the secondary tier). Aside from modeling all these dimensions simultaneously, the correlations between primary dimensions improve the accuracy of the item and person parameter estimates (L. Cai, 2010b). Thus, the two-tier model seems ideally suited for complex multidimensional assessment data.

The two-tier model can also be used to examine changes across time. Longitudinal data are collected by administering the same test to the same respondents across multiple occasions. For example, the effect of an intervention can be assessed by administering the same questionnaire at the start of an experiment and at the end (i.e., a pretest/posttest design). Although this type of analysis is commonplace, it is important to keep in mind that longitudinal item response data are likely to violate the local independence assumption due to administration of the same questions across time points.

112

Thus, when calibrating the item parameters for longitudinal IRT analysis, researchers typically use data from the first time point only (Hill, 2006).

An alternate strategy is to directly model the dependence between time points. In the two-tier model, the primary tier can be specified to represent multiple testing occasions, and the secondary tier can address the local item dependence that arises due to administering the same test across time points. Figure 9.2 illustrates such a model: The squares represent a set of six items that are administered at Time 1 (the large circle on the left) and again at Time 2 (the large circle on the right). The dependence between repeated administrations of each item is represented by the six small circles; for statistical identification of the model, the items within these "doublet" factors would be constrained to equality. Note that a key advantage of the two-tier approach to longitudinal IRT modeling is that the data from Time 1 and Time 2 can be pooled for item calibration, resulting in a larger overall sample size and thus more stable item parameter estimates.

In addition to the applications presented earlier, the two-tier model and its various extensions and adaptations have been used to model latent classes (Bacci & Bartolucci, 2016), multilevel multisite cluster randomized design data (L. Cai, Choi, Hansen, & Harrell, 2016), and other implementations. If we were to also consider the models that are nested within the two-tier structure (see Chapter 6), we would uncover an impressive number and diversity of MIRT applications.

Figure 9.2 Two-tier specification for longitudinal data.

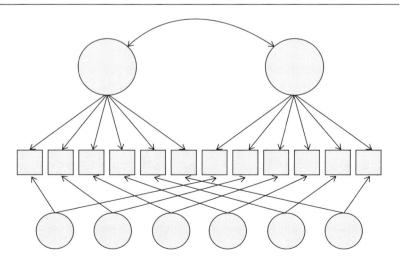

Further MIRT Applications

Although a comprehensive list would be overwhelming, a casual review of recent MIRT applications includes the estimation of student growth percentiles (Monroe & Cai, 2015) and response styles (Bolt, Lu, & Kim, 2014; Falk & Cai, 2016a); dimensionality assessment (Gnaldi, 2017) and the use of MIRT in creating unidimensional tests (Stucky & Edelen, 2015); and models for ipsative data (Brown & Maydeu-Olivares, 2013), missing data (Bacci & Bartolucci, 2013; Rose, von Davier, & Nagengast, 2017), answer-until-correct assessments (Culpepper, 2014), and rating data from multiple informants (Bauer et al., 2013). Clearly, the sophistication and flexibility of the MIRT modeling framework permits myriad opportunities for psychometric innovation.

Aside from the countless MIRT applications that have been proposed in the measurement literature, we were also unable to discuss various cutting-edge MIRT-related methods such as explanatory MIRT models that explain, rather than describe, the model parameters (De Boeck & Wilson, 2015), multilevel IRT models for nested data (Fox & Glas, 2001), mixture MIRT models that incorporate covariates (Finch & Hernández Finch, 2013), and nonparametric MIRT models that do not rely on the standard models presented in this text (Hojtink & Molenaar, 1997). Indeed, the psychometric literature is brimming with MIRT modeling advancements that expand upon the concepts and methods presented in the book. Interested readers can stay up-to-date on the latest technical and applied aspects of MIRT by browsing journals such as *Psychometrika, Multivariate Behavioral Research, Journal of Educational and Behavioral Statistics, Psychological Methods, Applied Psychological Measurement,* and others.

REFERENCES

Ackerman, T. A. (1996). Graphical representation of multidimensional item response theory analyses. *Applied Psychological Measurement, 20,* 311–330.

Ackerman, T. A., Gierl, M. J., & Walker, C. M. (2003). Using multidimensional item response theory to evaluate educational and psychological tests. *Educational Measurement: Issues and Practice, 22*(3), 37–51.

Ackerman, T. A., & Turner, R. (2003, April). *Estimation and application of a generalized MIRT model: Assessing the degree of compensation between two latent abilities.* Paper presented at the annual meeting of the National Council on Measurement in Education, Chicago.

Adams, R. J., Wilson, M., & Wang, W. C. (1997). The multidimensional random coefficients multinomial logit model. *Applied Psychological Measurement, 21*(1), 1–23.

Akaike, H. (1974). A new look at the statistical model identification. *IEEE Transactions on Automatic Control, 19*(6), 716–723.

Albert, J. H. (1992). Bayesian estimation of normal ogive item response curves using Gibbs sampling. *Journal of Educational Statistics, 17*(3), 251–269.

Albert, J. H., & Chib, S. (1993). Bayesian analysis of binary and polychotomous response data. *Theory and Methods, 88*(422), 669–679.

Andersen, E. B. (1985). Estimating latent correlations between repeated testings. *Psychometrika, 50,* 3–16.

Andrich, D. (1978). A rating formulation for ordered response categories. *Psychometrika, 43*(4), 561–573.

Bacci, S., & Bartolucci, F. (2016). Two-tier latent class IRT models in R. *The R Journal, 8*(2), 139–166.

Baker, F. B., & Kim, S. H. (2004). *Item response theory: Parameter estimation techniques.* Boca Raton, FL: CRC Press.

Bartholomew, D. J., & Tzamourani, P. (1999). The goodness of fit of latent trait models in attitude measurement. *Sociological Methods & Research, 27*(4), 525–546.

116

Bartolucci, F. (2007). A class of multidimensional IRT models for testing unidimensionality and clustering items. *Psychometrika*, *72*(2), 141–157.

Barton, M. A., & Lord, F. M. (1981). An upper asymptote for the three-parameter logistic item-response model. *ETS Research Report Series*, *1981*(1), i–8.

Bashkov, B. M., & DeMars, C. E. (2017). Examining the performance of the Metropolis–Hastings Robbins–Monro algorithm in the estimation of multilevel multidimensional IRT models. *Applied Psychological Measurement*, *41*(5), 323–337.

Bauer, D. J., Howard, A. L., Baldasaro, R. E., Curran, P. J., Hussong, A. M., Chassin, L., & Zucker, R. A. (2013). A trifactor model for integrating ratings across multiple informants. *Psychological Methods*, *18*(4), 475–493.

Bayes, T. (1763). An essay towards solving a problem in the doctrine of chances. *Philosophical Transactions of the Royal Society of London*, *53*, 370–418.

Béguin, A. A., & Glas, C. A. (2001). MCMC estimation and some model-fit analysis of multidimensional IRT models. *Psychometrika*, *66*(4), 541–561.

Birnbaum, A. (1968). Some latent trait models and their use in inferring an examinee's ability. In F. M. Lord & M. R. Novick (Eds.), *Statistical theories of mental test scores* (pp. 397–472). Reading, MA: Addison-Wesley.

Bock, R. D. (1972). Estimating item parameters and latent ability when responses are scored in two or more nominal categories. *Psychometrika*, *37*(1), 29–51.

Bock, R. D., & Aitkin, M. (1981). Marginal maximum likelihood estimation of item parameters: Application of an EM algorithm. *Psychometrika*, *46*(4), 443–459.

Bock, R. D., Gibbons, R., & Muraki, E. (1988). Full-information item factor analysis. *Applied Psychological Measurement*, *12*(3), 261–280.

Bock, R. D., & Lieberman, M. (1970). Fitting a response model for *n* dichotomously scored items. *Psychometrika*, *35*(2), 179–197.

Bolt, D. M., & Johnson, T. R. (2009). Addressing score bias and differential item functioning due to individual differences in response style. *Applied Psychological Measurement*, *33*(5), 335–352.

Bolt, D. M., & Lall, V. F. (2003). Estimation of compensatory and noncompensatory multidimensional item response models using Markov chain Monte Carlo. *Applied Psychological Measurement*, *27*(6), 395–414.

Bolt, D. M., Lu, Y., & Kim, J. S. (2014). Measurement and control of response styles using anchoring vignettes: A model-based approach. *Psychological Methods*, *19*(4), 528–541.

Bonifay, W. (2015). An illustration of the full-information two-tier item factor analysis model. In S. P. Reise & D. A. Revicki (Eds.), *Handbook of item response theory modeling: Applications to typical performance assessment* (pp. 207–225). New York: Routledge.

Bonifay, W., & Cai, L. (2017). On the complexity of item response theory models. *Multivariate Behavioral Research*, *52*(4), 465–484.

Bonifay, W., Lane, S. P., & Reise, S. P. (2017). Three concerns with applying a bifactor model as a structure of psychopathology. *Clinical Psychological Science*, *5*(1), 184–186.

Bradlow, E. T., Wainer, H., & Wang, X. (1999). A Bayesian random effects model for testlets. *Psychometrika*, *64*(2), 153–168.

Bradshaw, L., Izsák, A., Templin, J., & Jacobson, E. (2014). Diagnosing teachers' understandings of rational numbers: Building a multidimensional test within the diagnostic classification framework. *Educational Measurement: Issues and Practice*, *33*(1), 2–14.

Braeken, J. (2011). A boundary mixture approach to violations of conditional independence. *Psychometrika*, *76*(1), 57–76.

Briggs, D. C., & Wilson, M. (2003). An introduction to multidimensional measurement using Rasch models. *Journal of Applied Measurement*, *4*, 87–100.

Brown, A., & Maydeu-Olivares, A. (2013). How IRT can solve problems of ipsative data in forced-choice questionnaires. *Psychological Methods*, *18*(1), 36–52.

Buchholz, J., & Hartig, J. (2018). The impact of ignoring the partially compensatory relation between ability dimensions on norm-referenced test scores. *Psychological Test and Assessment Modeling*, *60*(3), 369–385.

Bulus, M., & Bonifay, W. (2016). irtDemo: Item response theory demo collection [Computer software] (R package version 0.1.2)./

Cagnone, S., & Monari, P. (2013). Latent variable models for ordinal data by using the adaptive quadrature approximation. *Computational Statistics*, *28*(2), 597–619.

Cai, L. (2008). SEM of another flavour: Two new applications of the supplemented EM algorithm. *British Journal of Mathematical and Statistical Psychology*, *61*(2), 309–329.

Cai, L. (2010a). Metropolis-Hastings Robbins-Monro algorithm for confirmatory item factor analysis. *Journal of Educational and Behavioral Statistics*, *35*(3), 307–335.

Cai, L. (2010b). A two-tier full-information item factor analysis model with applications. *Psychometrika*, *75*(4), 581–612.

Cai, L., Choi, K., Hansen, M., & Harrell, L. (2016). Item response theory. *Annual Review of Statistics and Its Application*, *3*, 297–321.

Cai, L., & Hansen, M. (2013). Limited-information goodness-of-fit testing of hierarchical item factor models. *British Journal of Mathematical and Statistical Psychology*, *66*(2), 245–276.

Cai, L., & Hansen, M. (2017). Improving educational assessment: Multivariate statistical methods. *Policy Insights From the Behavioral and Brain Sciences*, *5*(1), 19–24.

Cai, L., Maydeu-Olivares, A., Coffman, D. L., & Thissen, D. (2006). Limited-information goodness-of-fit testing of item response theory models for sparse 2^P tables. *British Journal of Mathematical and Statistical Psychology*, *59*(1), 173–194.

Cai, L., & Thissen, D. (2015). Modern approaches to parameter estimation in item response theory. In S. P. Reise & D. A. Revicki (Eds.), *Handbook of item response theory modeling: Applications to typical performance assessment* (pp. 41–59). New York: Routledge.

Cai, Y. (2015). The value of using test response data for content validity: An application of the bifactor-MIRT to a nursing knowledge test. *Nurse Education Today*, *35*(12), 1181–1185.

Carpenter, B., Gelman, A., Hoffman, M. D., Lee, D., Goodrich, B., Betancourt, M., Brubaker, M. A., Guo, J., Li, P., & Riddell, A. (2017). Stan: A probabilistic programming language. *Journal of Statistical Software*, *76*(1), 1–32.

Chalmers, R. P. (2012). mirt: A multidimensional item response theory package for the R environment. *Journal of Statistical Software*, *48*(6), 1–29.

Chalmers, R. P. (2015). Extended mixed-effects item response models with the MH-RM algorithm. *Journal of Educational Measurement*, *52*(2), 200–222.

Chalmers, R. P., & Flora, D. B. (2014). Maximum-likelihood estimation of noncompensatory IRT models with the MH-RM algorithm. *Applied Psychological Measurement, 38*(5), 339–358.

Chen, C. Y., Xie, H., Clifford, J., Chen, C. I., & Squires, J. (2018). Examining internal structures of a developmental measure using multidimensional item response theory. *Journal of Early Intervention, 40*(4), 287–303.

Chen, J., & de la Torre, J. (2014). A procedure for diagnostically modeling extant large-scale assessment data: The case of the programme for international student assessment in reading. *Psychology, 5*(18), 1967–1978.

Chen, W. H., & Thissen, D. (1997). Local dependence indexes for item pairs using item response theory. *Journal of Educational and Behavioral Statistics, 22*(3), 265–289.

Colledani, D., Anselmi, P., & Robusto, E. (2019). Using multidimensional item response theory to develop an abbreviated form of the Italian version of Eysenck's IVE questionnaire. *Personality and Individual Differences, 142*, 45–52.

Culpepper, S. A. (2014). If at first you don't succeed, try, try again: Applications of sequential IRT models to cognitive assessments. *Applied Psychological Measurement, 38*(8), 632–644.

Culpepper, S. A. (2017). The prevalence and implications of slipping on low-stakes, large-scale assessments. *Journal of Educational and Behavioral Statistics, 42*(6), 706–725.

de Ayala, R. J. (1994). The influence of multidimensionality on the graded response model. *Applied Psychological Measurement, 18*(2), 155–170.

de Ayala, R. J. (2009). *The theory and practice of item response theory.* New York: Guilford.

De Boeck, P., & Wilson, M. (2015). Multidimensional explanatory item response modeling. In S. P. Reise & D. A. Revicki (Eds.), *Handbook of item response theory modeling: Applications to typical performance assessment* (pp. 252–271). New York: Routledge.

de la Torre, J., & Douglas, J. A. (2004). Higher-order latent trait models for cognitive diagnosis. *Psychometrika, 69*(3), 333–353.

de la Torre, J., van der Ark, L. A., & Rossi, G. (2015). Analysis of clinical data from a cognitive diagnosis modeling framework. *Measurement and Evaluation in Counseling and Development, 51*(4), 281–296.

DeMars, C. E. (2013). A tutorial on interpreting bifactor model scores. *International Journal of Testing*, *13*(4), 354–378.

DeMars, C. E. (2016). Partially compensatory multidimensional item response theory models: two alternate model forms. *Educational and Psychological Measurement*, *76*(2), 231–257.

Dempster, A. P., Laird, N. M., & Rubin, D. B. (1977). Maximum likelihood from incomplete data via the EM algorithm. *Journal of the Royal Statistical Society, Series B (Methodological)*, *39*(1), 1–38.

DeSimone, J. A., & James, L. R. (2015). An item analysis of the Conditional Reasoning Test of Aggression. *Journal of Applied Psychology*, *100*(6), 1872–1886.

Desjardins, C. D., & Bulut, O. (2018). *Handbook of educational measurement and psychometrics using R*. Boca Raton, FL: CRC Press.

DiTrapani, J., Rockwood, N., & Jeon, M. (2018). Explanatory IRT analysis using the SPIRIT macro in SPSS. *Tutorials in Quantitative Methods for Psychology*, *14*(2), 81–98.

Dorans, N. J., & Holland, P. W. (2000). Population invariance and the equatability of tests: Basic theory and the linear case. *Journal of Educational Measurement*, *37*(4), 281–306.

Embretson, S. E. (1991). A multidimensional latent trait model for measuring learning and change. *Psychometrika*, *56*(3), 495–515.

Embretson, S. E., & Reise, S. P. (2000). *Item response theory*. New York: Psychology Press.

Falk, C. F., & Cai, L. (2016a). A flexible full-information approach to the modeling of response styles. *Psychological Methods*, *21*(3), 328–347.

Falk, C. F., & Cai, L. (2016b). Maximum marginal likelihood estimation of a monotonic polynomial generalized partial credit model with applications to multiple group analysis. *Psychometrika*, *81*(2), 434–460.

Falk, C. F., & Cai, L. (2016c). Semiparametric item response functions in the context of guessing. *Journal of Educational Measurement*, *53*(2), 229–247.

Finch, W. H., & Hernández Finch, M. E. (2013). Investigation of specific learning disability and testing accommodations based differential item functioning using a multilevel multidimensional mixture item response theory model. *Educational and Psychological Measurement*, *73*(6), 973–993.

Fisher, R. A. (1925). Theory of statistical estimation. *Proceedings of the Cambridge Philosophical Society*, *22*(5), 700–725.

Fletcher, R., & Hattie, J. (2005). Gender differences in physical self-concept: A multidimensional differential item functioning analysis. *Educational and Psychological Measurement*, *65*(4), 657–667.

Fox, J.-P. (2010). *Bayesian item response modeling: Theory and applications*. New York: Springer.

Fox, J.-P., & Glas, C. A. (2001). Bayesian estimation of a multilevel IRT model using Gibbs sampling. *Psychometrika*, *66*(2), 271–288.

Fukuhara, H., & Kamata, A. (2011). A bifactor multidimensional item response theory model for differential item functioning analysis on testlet-based items. *Applied Psychological Measurement*, *35*(8), 604–622.

Gelfand, A. E. (1996). Model determination using sampling-based methods. In W. R. Gilks, S. Richardson, & D. J. Spiegelhalter (Eds.), *Markov chain Monte Carlo in practice* (pp. 145–161). Boca Raton, FL: Chapman & Hall/CRC.

Gibbons, R. D., & Hedeker, D. R. (1992). Full-information item bi-factor analysis. *Psychometrika*, *57*(3), 423–436.

Gibbons, R. D., Rush, A. J., & Immekus, J. C. (2009). On the psychometric validity of the domains of the PDSQ: An illustration of the bi-factor item response theory model. *Journal of Psychiatric Research*, *43*(4), 401–410.

Gnaldi, M. (2017). A multidimensional IRT approach for dimensionality assessment of standardised students' tests in mathematics. *Quality & Quantity*, *51*(3), 1167–1182.

Gulliksen, H. (1950). *Theory of mental tests*. New York: Routledge.

Haebara, T. (1980). Equating logistic ability scales by a weighted least squares method. *Japanese Psychological Research, 22*, 144–149.

Haertel, E. H. (1989). Using restricted latent class models to map the skill structure of achievement items. *Journal of Educational Measurement*, *26*(4), 301–321.

Hansen, M., Cai, L., Monroe, S., & Li, Z. (2016). Limited-information goodness-of-fit testing of diagnostic classification item response models. *British Journal of Mathematical and Statistical Psychology*, *69*(3), 225–252.

Hartig, J., & Harsch, C. (2017). Multidimensional structures of competencies: Focusing on text comprehension in English as a foreign language. In D. Leutner, J. Fleischer, J. Grünkorn, & E. Klieme (Eds.), *Competence assessment in education: Research, models, and instruments* (pp. 357–368). Cham, Switzerland: Springer.

Hartwell, M. R., Baker, F. B., & Zwarts, M. (1988). Item parameter estimation via maximum marginal likelihood and an EM algorithm: A didactic. *Journal of Educational and Behavioral Statistics, 13*(3), 243–271.

Hill, C. D. (2006). *Two models for longitudinal item response data.* Unpublished doctoral dissertation, University of North Carolina, Chapel Hill.

Hojtink, H., & Molenaar, I. W. (1997). A multidimensional item response model: Constrained latent class analysis using the Gibbs sampler and posterior predictive checks. *Psychometrika, 62*(2), 171–189.

Holland, P. W., & Thayer, D. T. (1988). Differential item performance and the Mantel-Haenszel procedure. In H. Wainer & H. I. Braun (Eds.), *Test validity* (pp. 129–145). Hillsdale, NJ: Lawrence Erlbaum.

Holzinger, K. J., & Swineford, F. (1937). The bi-factor method. *Psychometrika, 2*(1), 41–54.

Huebner, A., & Wang, C. (2011). A note on comparing examinee classification methods for cognitive diagnosis models. *Educational and Psychological Measurement, 71*(2), 407–419.

Jank, W. (2005). Quasi-Monte Carlo sampling to improve the efficiency of Monte Carlo EM. *Computational Statistics & Data Analysis, 48*(4), 685–701.

Jeon, M., Rijmen, F., & Rabe-Hesketh, S. (2014). Flexible item response theory modeling with FLIRT. *Applied Psychological Methods, 38*, 404–405.

Junker, B. W., & Sijtsma, K. (2001). Cognitive assessment models with few assumptions, and connections with nonparametric item response theory. *Applied Psychological Measurement, 25*(3), 258–272.

Jurich, D. P., & Bradshaw, L. P. (2013). An illustration of diagnostic classification modeling in student learning outcomes assessment. *International Journal of Testing, 14*(1), 49–72.

Kelderman, H. (1996). Multidimensional Rasch models for partial-credit scoring. *Applied Psychological Measurement, 20*(2), 155–168.

Kilgus, S. P., Bonifay, W. E., von der Embse, N. P., Allen, A. N., & Eklund, K. (2018). Evidence for the interpretation of Social, Academic, and Emotional Behavior Risk Screener (SAEBRS) scores: An argument-based approach to screener validation. *Journal of School Psychology*, *68*, 129–141.

Kolva, E., Rosenfeld, B., Liu, Y., Pessin, H., & Breitbart, W. (2017). Using item response theory (IRT) to reduce patient burden when assessing desire for hastened death. *Psychological Assessment, 29*(3), 349–353.

Lee, S., & Bolt, D. M. (2017). Asymmetric item characteristic curves and item complexity: Insights from simulation and real data analyses. *Psychometrika, 83*(2), 453–475.

Lee, S., & Bolt, D. M. (2018). An alternative to the 3PL: Using asymmetric item characteristic curves to address guessing effects. *Journal of Educational Measurement, 55*(1), 90–111.

Lee, S., Bulut, O., & Suh, Y. (2017). Multidimensional extension of multiple indicators multiple causes models to detect DIF. *Educational and Psychological Measurement, 77*(4), 545–569.

Lee, Y. S., Park, Y. S., & Taylan, D. (2011). A cognitive diagnostic modeling of attribute mastery in Massachusetts, Minnesota, and the US national sample using the TIMSS 2007. *International Journal of Testing, 11*(2), 144–177.

Levy, R., & Svetina, D. (2011). A generalized dimensionality discrepancy measure for dimensionality assessment in multidimensional item response theory. *British Journal of Mathematical and Statistical Psychology, 64*(2), 208–232.

Li, Y., Bolt, D. M., & Fu, J. (2006). A comparison of alternative models for testlets. *Applied Psychological Measurement, 30*(1), 3–21.

Li, Y., Li, S., & Wang, L. (2010). Application of a general polytomous testlet model to the reading section of a large-scale English language assessment. *ETS Research Report Series, 2010*(2), i–34.

Lin, T. H., & Dayton, C. M. (1997). Model selection information criteria for non-nested latent class models. *Journal of Educational and Behavioral Statistics, 22*(3), 249–264.

Linacre, J. M. (1999). Understanding Rasch measurement: Estimation methods for Rasch measures. *Journal of Outcome Measurement, 3*(4), 382–405.

Little, R. J., & Rubin, D. B. (2014). *Statistical analysis with missing data.* New York: Wiley.

Lord, F. M. (1980). *Applications of item response theory to practical testing problems.* Hillside, NJ: Lawrence Erlbaum.

Lucke, J. F. (2014). Positive trait item response models. In R. E. Millsap, L. A. van der Ark, D. M. Bolt, & C. M. Woods (Eds.), *New developments in quantitative psychology: Presentations from the 77th annual Psychometric Society meeting.* New York: Springer.

Lucke, J. F. (2015). Unipolar item response models. In S. P. Reise & D. A. Revicki (Eds.), *Handbook of item response theory modeling: Applications to typical performance assessment* (pp. 272–284). New York: Routledge.

Ma, W., & de la Torre, J. (2019). GDINA: The generalized DINA model framework [Computer software] (R package version 2.5).

Magis, D. (2013). A note on the item information function of the four-parameter logistic model. *Applied Psychological Measurement, 37*(4), 304–315.

Magis, D. (2015). A note on the equivalence between observed and expected information functions with polytomous IRT models. *Journal of Educational and Behavioral Statistics, 40*(1), 96–105.

Maris, E. (1999). Estimating multiple classification latent class models. *Psychometrika, 64*(2), 187–212.

Martín-Fernández, M., & Revuelta, J. (2017). Bayesian estimation of multidimensional item response models: A comparison of analytic and simulation algorithms. *Psicológica, 38*, 25–55.

Masters, G. N. (1982). A Rasch model for partial credit scoring. *Psychometrika, 47*(2), 149–174.

Maydeu-Olivares, A. (2013). Goodness-of-fit assessment of item response theory models. *Measurement: Interdisciplinary Research and Perspectives, 11*(3), 71–101.

Maydeu-Olivares, A., & Cai, L. (2006). A cautionary note on using G^2(dif) to assess relative model fit in categorical data analysis. *Multivariate Behavioral Research, 41*(1), 55–64.

Maydeu-Olivares, A., Hernández, A., & McDonald, R. P. (2006). A multidimensional ideal point item response theory model for binary data. *Multivariate Behavioral Research, 41*(4), 445–472.

Maydeu-Olivares, A., & Joe, H. (2005). Limited- and full-information estimation and goodness-of-fit testing in 2^n contingency tables: A unified framework. *Journal of the American Statistical Association, 100*(471), 1009–1020.

Maydeu-Olivares, A., & Joe, H. (2006). Limited information goodness-of-fit testing in multidimensional contingency tables. *Psychometrika, 71*(4), 713–732.

Maydeu-Olivares, A., & Joe, H. (2014). Assessing approximate fit in categorical data analysis. *Multivariate Behavioral Research, 49*(4), 305–328.

McDonald, R. P. (1997). Normal-ogive multidimensional model. In W. J. van der Linden & R. K. Hambleton (Eds.), *Handbook of modern item response theory* (pp. 257–269). New York: Springer.

McKinley, R. L., & Way, W. D. (1992). The feasibility of modeling secondary TOEFL ability dimensions using multidimensional IRT models. *ETS Research Report Series, 1992*(1), i–22.

Meng, X. L., & Schilling, S. (1996). Fitting full-information item factor models and an empirical investigation of bridge sampling. *Journal of the American Statistical Association, 91*(435), 1254–1267.

Monroe, S., & Cai, L. (2015). Examining the reliability of student growth percentiles using multidimensional IRT. *Educational Measurement: Issues and Practice, 34*(4), 21–30.

Morris, S., Bass, M., Lee, M., & Neapolitan, R. E. (2017). Advancing the efficiency and efficacy of patient reported outcomes with multivariate computer adaptive testing. *Journal of the American Medical Informatics Association: JAMIA, 24*(5), 897–902.

Mroch, A. A., & Bolt, D. M. (2006). A simulation comparison of parametric and nonparametric dimensionality detection procedures. *Applied Measurement in Education, 19*(1), 67–91.

Mulaik, S. A. (1972). *The foundations of factor analysis.* New York: McGraw-Hill.

Muraki, E. (1992). A generalized partial credit model: Application of an EM algorithm. *ETS Research Report Series, 1992*(1), i–30.

Muraki, E., & Carlson, J. E. (1995). Full-information factor analysis for polytomous item responses. *Applied Psychological Measurement, 19*(1), 73–90.

Muthén, B., & Asparouhov, T. (2012). Bayesian structural equation modeling: A more flexible representation of substantive theory. *Psychological Methods*, *17*(3), 313–335.

Muthén, L. K., & Muthén, B. O. (2017). *Mplus user's guide* (8th ed.). Los Angeles: Author.

Naylor, J. C., & Smith, A. F. (1982). Applications of a method for the efficient computation of posterior distributions. *Applied Statistics*, *31*, 214–225.

O'Connor, S. S., Comtois, K. A., Atkins, D. C., & Kerbrat, A. H. (2017). Examining the impact of suicide attempt function and perceived effectiveness in predicting reattempt for emergency medicine patients. *Behavior Therapy*, *48*(1), 45–55.

Orlando, M., & Thissen, D. (2000). Likelihood-based item-fit indices for dichotomous item response theory models. *Applied Psychological Measurement*, *24*(1), 50–64.

Orlando, M., & Thissen, D. (2003). Further investigation of the performance of S-X^2: An item fit index for use with dichotomous item response theory models. *Applied Psychological Measurement*, *27*(4), 289–298.

Preston, K., Reise, S., Cai, L., & Hays, R. D. (2011). Using the nominal response model to evaluate response category discrimination in the PROMIS emotional distress item pools. *Educational and Psychological Measurement*, *71*(3), 523–550.

Pretz, C. R., Kean, J., Heinemann, A. W., Kozlowski, A. J., Bode, R. K., & Gebhardt, E. (2016). A multidimensional Rasch analysis of the Functional Independence Measure based on the National Institute on Disability, Independent Living, and Rehabilitation Research Traumatic Brain Injury Model Systems National Database. *Journal of Neurotrauma*, *33*(14), 1358–1362.

R Core Team. (2018). *R: A language and environment for statistical computing*. Vienna, Austria: R Foundation for Statistical Computing.

Rabe-Hesketh, S., Skrondal, A., & Pickles, A. (2002). Reliable estimation of generalized linear mixed models using adaptive quadrature. *The Stata Journal*, *2*(1), 1–21.

Rasch, G. (1960). *Probabilistic models for some intelligence and attainment tests*. Chicago: University of Chicago Press.

Ravand, H. (2016). Application of a cognitive diagnostic model to a high-stakes reading comprehension test. *Journal of Psychoeducational Assessment, 34*(8), 782–799.

Ravand, H., Barati, H., & Widhiarso, W. (2013). Exploring diagnostic capacity of a high stakes reading comprehension test: A pedagogical demonstration. *Iranian Journal of Language Testing, 3*(1), 12–37.

Reckase, M. D. (1997). A linear logistic multidimensional model for dichotomous item response data. In *Handbook of modern item response theory* (pp. 271–286). Springer, New York, NY.

Reckase, M. D. (2009). *Multidimensional item response theory*. New York: Springer.

Reise, S. P. (2012). The rediscovery of bifactor measurement models. *Multivariate Behavioral Research, 47*(5), 667–696.

Reise, S. P., Morizot, J., & Hays, R. D. (2007). The role of the bifactor model in resolving dimensionality issues in health outcomes measures. *Quality of Life Research, 16*(1), 19–31.

Reiser, M. (1996). Analysis of residuals for the multinomial item response model. *Psychometrika, 61*(3), 509–528.

Revuelta, J. (2014). Multidimensional item response model for nominal variables. *Applied Psychological Measurement, 38*, 549–562.

Rizopoulos, D., & Moustaki, I. (2008). Generalized latent variable models with non-linear effects. *British Journal of Mathematical and Statistical Psychology, 61*(2), 415–438.

Robitzsch, A. (2019). sirt: Supplementary item response theory models [Computer software] (R package version 3.5-53).

Robitzsch, A., Kiefer, T., George, A. C., & Uenlue, A. (2017). CDM: Cognitive diagnosis modeling (R package version 7.2-30).

Rodriguez, A., Reise, S. P., & Haviland, M. G. (2016). Evaluating bifactor models: Calculating and interpreting statistical indices. *Psychological Methods, 21*(2), 137–150.

Rose, N., von Davier, M., & Nagengast, B. (2017). Modeling omitted and not-reached items in IRT models. *Psychometrika, 82*(3), 795–819.

Roussos, L. A., & Ozbek, O. Y. (2006). Formulation of the DETECT population parameter and evaluation of DETECT estimator bias. *Journal of Educational Measurement*, *43*(3), 215–243.

Rupp, A. A., Templin, J., & Henson, R. A. (2010). *Diagnostic measurement: Theory, methods, and applications*. New York: Guilford.

Sam, K. L., Li, C., & Lo, S. K. (2016). Validation of the Mental Retardation Attitude Inventory-Revised (MRAI-R): A multidimensional Rasch analysis. *International Journal of Social Science and Humanity*, *6*(7), 519–524.

Samejima, F. (1969). *Estimation of latent ability using a response pattern of graded scores*. (Psychometrika Monograph Supplement, No. 17*)*. Richmond, VA: Psychometric Society.

SAS Institute Inc. (2015). *SAS/IML® 14.1 user's guide*. Cary, NC: Author.

Schilling, S., & Bock, R. D. (2005). High-dimensional maximum marginal likelihood item factor analysis by adaptive quadrature. *Psychometrika*, *70*(3), 533–555.

Schwarz, G. (1978). Estimating the dimension of a model. *Annals of Statistics*, *6*(2), 461–464.

Shealy, R., & Stout, W. (1993). A model-based standardization approach that separates true bias/DIF from group ability differences and detects test bias/DTF as well as item bias/DIF. *Psychometrika*, *58*(2), 159–194.

Sijtsma, K., & Molenaar, I. W. (2002). *Introduction to nonparametric item response theory*. Thousand Oaks, CA: Sage.

Simms, L. J., Grös, D. F., Watson, D., & O'Hara, M. W. (2008). Parsing the general and specific components of depression and anxiety with bifactor modeling. *Depression and Anxiety*, *25*(7), E34–E46.

Spiegelhalter, D. J., Best, N. G., Carlin, B. P., & van der Linde, A. (2002). Bayesian measures of model complexity and fit. *Journal of the Royal Statistical Society: Series B (Statistical Methodology)*, *64*(4), 583–639.

Spray, J. A., Ackerman, T. A., & Carlson, J. (1986). *An analysis of multidimensional item response theory models*. Paper presented at the annual meeting of the Office of Naval Research Contractors, Gatlinburg, TN.

Stan Development Team. (2018). RStan: The R interface to Stan [Computer software] (R package version 2.17.3). Retrieved from http://mc-stan.org/

Stocking, M. L., & Lord, F. M. (1983). Developing a common metric in item response theory. *Applied Psychological Measurement, 7*(2), 201–210.

Stout, W. (1987). A nonparametric approach for assessing latent trait unidimensionality. *Psychometrika, 52*, 589–617.

Stout, W., Habing, B., Douglas, J., Kim, H. R., Roussos, L., & Zhang, J. (1996). Conditional covariance-based nonparametric multidimensionality assessment. *Applied Psychological Measurement, 20*(4), 331–354.

Stout, W. F. (1990). A new item response theory modeling approach with applications to unidimensionality assessment and ability estimation. *Psychometrika, 55*(2), 293–325.

Stucky, B. D., & Edelen, M. O. (2015). Using hierarchical IRT models to create unidimensional measures from multidimensional data. In S. P. Reise & D. A. Revicki (Eds.), *Handbook of item response theory modeling: Applications to typical performance assessment* (pp. 183–206). New York: Routledge.

Svetina, D., & Levy, R. (2012). An overview of software for conducting dimensionality assessment in multidimensional models. *Applied Psychological Measurement, 36*(8), 659–669.

Sympson, J. B. (1978). A model for testing with multidimensional items. In D. J. Weiss (Ed.), *Proceedings of the 1977 computerized adaptive testing conference* (pp. 82–98). Minneapolis: University of Minnesota, Department of Psychology, Psychometric Methods Program.

Tatsuoka, K. K. (1983). Rule space: An approach for dealing with misconceptions based on item response theory. *Journal of Educational Measurement, 20*(4), 345–354.

Thissen, D., Cai, L., & Bock, R. D. (2010). The nominal categories item response model. In M. Nering & R. Ostini (Eds.), *Handbook of polytomous item response theory models: Developments and applications* (pp. 43–75). New York: Taylor & Francis.

Thissen, D., & Steinberg, L. (1986). A taxonomy of item response models. *Psychometrika, 51*(4), 567–577.

Thissen, D., & Wainer, H. (Eds.). (2001). *Test scoring*. New York: Routledge.

Thomas, M. L. (2012). Rewards of bridging the divide between measurement and clinical theory: Demonstration of a bifactor model for the Brief Symptom Inventory. *Psychological Assessment, 24*(1), 101–113.

Thurstone, L. L. (1947). *Multiple factor analysis*. Chicago: University of Chicago Press.

Toland, M. D., Sulis, I., Giambona, F., Porcu, M., & Campbell, J. M. (2017). Introduction to bifactor polytomous item response theory analysis. *Journal of School Psychology*, *60*, 41–63.

van der Linden, W. J., & Glas, C. A. (Eds.). (2000). *Computerized adaptive testing: Theory and practice*. Dordrecht: Kluwer Academic.

van Rijn, P. W., Sinharay, S., Haberman, S. J., & Johnson, M. S. (2016). Assessment of fit of item response theory models used in large-scale educational survey assessments. *Large-Scale Assessments in Education*, *4*(1), 1–23.

Wainer, H., Bradlow, E. T., & Wang, X. (2007). *Testlet response theory and its applications*. New York: Cambridge University Press.

Wainer, H., Dorans, N. J., Flaugher, R., Green, B. F., & Mislevy, R. J. (2000). *Computerized adaptive testing: A primer*. New York: Routledge.

Walker, C. M., Zhang, B., & Surber, J. (2008). Using a multidimensional differential item functioning framework to determine if reading ability affects student performance in mathematics. *Applied Measurement in Education*, *21*(2), 162–181.

Wang, X., Bradlow, E. T., Wainer, H., & Muller, E. S. (2008). A Bayesian method for studying DIF: A cautionary tale filled with surprises and delights. *Journal of Educational and Behavioral Statistics*, *33*(3), 363–384.

Weeks, J. P. (2015). Multidimensional test linking. In S. P. Reise & D. A. Revicki (Eds.), *Handbook of item response theory modeling: Applications to typical performance assessment* (pp. 406–434). New York: Routledge.

Wei, G. C., & Tanner, M. A. (1990). A Monte Carlo implementation of the EM algorithm and the poor man's data augmentation algorithms. *Journal of the American Statistical Association*, *85*(411), 699–704.

Wetzel, E., & Hell, B. (2014). Multidimensional item response theory models in vocational interest measurement: An illustration using the AIST-R. *Journal of Psychoeducational Assessment*, *32*(4), 342–355.

Yang, J. S., & Cai, L. (2014). Estimation of contextual effects through nonlinear multilevel latent variable modeling with a Metropolis–Hastings Robbins–Monro algorithm. *Journal of Educational and Behavioral Statistics*, *39*(6), 550–582.

Yao, L., & Schwarz, R. D. (2006). A multidimensional partial credit model with associated item and test statistics: An application to mixed-format tests. *Applied Psychological Measurement, 30*(6), 469–492.

Yen, W. M. (1984). Effects of local item dependence on the fit and equating performance of the three-parameter logistic model. *Applied Psychological Measurement, 8*(2), 125–145.

Zhang, B., & Stone, C. A. (2008). Evaluating item fit for multidimensional item response models. *Educational and Psychological Measurement, 68*(2), 181–196.

Zhang, J. (2007). Conditional covariance theory and DETECT for polytomous items. *Psychometrika, 72*(1), 69–91.

Zhang, J., & Stout, W. (1999a). Conditional covariance structure of generalized compensatory multidimensional items. *Psychometrika, 64*(2), 129–152.

Zhang, J., & Stout, W. (1999b). The theoretical DETECT index of dimensionality and its application to approximate simple structure. *Psychometrika, 64*(2), 213–249.

Zheng, Y., Chang, C. H., & Chang, H. H. (2013). Content-balancing strategy in bifactor computerized adaptive patient-reported outcome measurement. *Quality of Life Research, 22*(3), 491–499.

INDEX

Ackerman, T. A., 75
Adaptive quadrature, and estimation in MIRT models, 88–89
Aitkin, M., 22–23, 87–88
Allen, A. N., 51
Applications of two-tier item factor structure, and MIRT application, 111–112
Asparouhov, T., 89
Asymmetric item response functions models, 17

Baker, F. B., 2, 84
Barton, M. A., 12, 13
Bayesian estimation
    estimation in MIRT models, 88, 89–90
    UIRT estimation methods, 22, 24, 26
Béguin, A. A., 90
Bifactor model, and item factor structures, 81
Bock, R. D., 14, 21, 22–23, 52–53, 87–88, 89
Bolt, D. M., 41, 54, 104
Bonifay, W., 51, 79
Bradlow, E. T., 81–82
Bradshaw, L. P., 44
Briggs, D. C., 3
Brown, A., 80
Buchholz, J., 38

Cagnone, S., 89
Cai, L., 52–53, 79, 80, 84, 89, 90
Campbell, J. M., 52

Carlson, J. E., 61, 66
CAT (computerized adaptive testing), and MIRT application, 109–110
Chen, C. I., 52
Chen, C. Y., 52
Clifford, J., 52
Compensation, in MIRT models for dichotomous data, 27–31
Compensatory MIRT models
    about, 31
    multidimensional 2-parameter logistic (M2PL) model, 31–34
    multidimensional 3-parameter logistic (M3PL) model, 34–35
    multidimensional 4-parameter logistic (M4PL) model, 35–36
    multidimensional Rasch model (MRM), 37
Computerized adaptive testing (CAT), and MIRT application, 109–110
Conceptual illustration, and estimation in MIRT models, 83–84
Conditional response functions, and descriptive MIRT statistics, 58–60
Correlated-traits model, and item factor structures, 80
Culpepper, S. A., 36

DeMars, C. E., 35
Dempster, A. P., 86

134

Descriptive MIRT statistics
  about, 3
  conditional response functions,
    58–60
  direction of measurement, 60–67
  item response surface, 57–58
  MIRT information, 70–71
  person parameters in MIRT,
    67–70
  polytomous MIRT descriptives,
    71–74
  test-level MIRT descriptives, 75
  θ-space, 55–56
DeSimone, J., 33
Diagnostic classification models,
    42–43
Dichotomous data models, 6–13.
    See also Chap 3 MIRT
    models for dichotomous
    data
Difference models, and polytomous
    data models, 14–15
Differential item functioning
    (DIF) MIRT application,
    107–109
Dimensionality assessment, and
    MIRT model diagnostics and
    evaluation, 93–97
Dimensionality assessment and
    use of MIRT in creating
    unidimensional tests, 113
Direction of measurement, and
    descriptive MIRT statistics,
    60–67
Divide-by-total models, and
    polytomous data models,
    15–16
Dorans, N. J., 107

Eklund, K., 51
EM algorithm estimation method,
    22–24

Estimation in MIRT models
  about, 3, 83
  adaptive quadrature, 88–89
  Bayesian estimation, 88, 89–91
  conceptual illustration, 83–84
  MH-RM algorithm, 90–91
  missing data formulation, 84–87
  problems, 87–88
  R code, 91
Estimation methods, and UIRT
  about, 17–21
  Bayesian estimation, 22, 24, 26
  EM algorithm, 22–24
  joint estimation of both person
    and item parameters,
    21–22
  Markov chain Monte Carlo
    simulation method, 26
  Rasch model, 26
  scoring, 24–26
Estimation of student growth
    percentiles and response
    styles MIRT application, 113
Explanatory MIRT models, 113

Fisher, R. A., 86–87
Fletcher, R., 109
Fox, J.-P., 84
Fukuhara, H., 108

Generalized multidimensional IRT
    (GMIRT) model, 42
Giambona, F., 52
Glas, C. A., 90
Graded response model (GRM)
    multidimensional graded
      response model, 47–51
    polytomous data models,
      14, 15

Haberman, S. J., 35
Hansen, M., 80, 89, 90

Harsch, C., 37
Hartig, J., 37, 38
Hattie, J., 109
Haviland, M. G., 81
Hell, B., 52
Holland, P. W., 107

Introductory item response theory
    (IRT), 1
Ipsative data and missing data
    models, and MIRT
    application, 113
Item factor copula model, 45
Item factor structures
    about, 3, 77
    bifactor model, 81
    correlated-traits model, 80
    R code, 82
    testlet response model, 81–82
    two-tier model, 77–80
Item-level fit assessment, and
    MIRT model diagnostics and
    evaluation, 101–103
Item response surface, and
    descriptive MIRT statistics,
    57–58

Joe, H., 99–100
Johnson, M. S., 35
Johnson, T. R., 54
Joint estimation of both person
    and item parameters
    estimation method,
    21–22
Jurich, D. P., 44

Kamata, A., 108
Kilgus, S. P., 51
Kim, S. H., 2, 84

Lall, V. F., 41, 104
Levy, R., 96

Li, C., 37
Li, S., 82
Li, Y., 82
Lieberman, M., 21
Linking and equating, and MIRT
    application, 105–107
Lo, S. K., 37
Lord, F. M., 12, 13, 108

M2PL (multidimensional
    2-parameter logistic) model,
    31–34
M3PL (multidimensional
    3-parameter logistic) model,
    34–35
M4PL (multidimensional
    4-parameter logistic) model,
    35–36
Markov chain Monte Carlo
    simulation method, 26
Martín-Fernández, M., 90
Maydeu-Olivares, A., 80, 98,
    99–100
McKinley, R. L., 35
MGPCM (multidimensional
    generalized partial credit
    model), 51–54
MH-RM algorithm, and estimation
    in MIRT models, 90–91
MIRT (multidimensional item
    response theory), 13–14
MIRT application
    about, 3, 105
    answer-until-correct
        assessments and rating
        data from multiple
        informants, 113
    applications of two-tier
        item factor structure,
        111–112
    computerized adaptive testing
        (CAT), 109–110

differential item functioning (DIF), 107–109

dimensionality assessment and use of MIRT in creating unidimensional tests, 113

estimation of student growth percentiles and response styles, 113

explanatory MIRT models, 113

ipsative data and missing data models, 113

linking and equating, 105–107

mixture MIRT models that incorporate covariates, 113

multilevel IRT models for nested data, 113

nonparametric MIRT models, 113

R code, 107, 109, 111

resources, 113

MIRT information, and descriptive MIRT statistics, 70–71

MIRT model diagnostics and evaluation

about, 3, 93

dimensionality assessment, 93–97

item-level fit assessment, 101–103

model comparison methods, 103–104

test-level fit assessment, 97–100

MIRT models for dichotomous data. *See also* Compensatory MIRT models

about, 3, 27, 41–42

compensation in, 27–31

diagnostic classification models, 42–43

generalized multidimensional IRT (GMIRT) model, 42

item factor copula model, 45

MIRT unfolding ("ideal point" or "proximity") model, 45

multidimensional latent class model, 45

partially compensatory MIRT models, 38–41

R code, 37–38, 41, 45

variable compensation models, 42

MIRT models for polytomous data

about, 3, 47

multidimensional generalized partial credit model (MGPCM), 51–54

multidimensional graded response model (GRM), 47–51

multidimensional random coefficients multinomial logit model, 54

multidimensional Rasch model, 54

R code, 54

MIRT unfolding ("ideal point" or "proximity") model, 45

Missing data formulation, and estimation in MIRT models, 84–87

Mixture MIRT models that incorporate covariates, 113

Model comparison methods, and MIRT model diagnostics and evaluation, 103–104

Monari, P., 89

Moustaki, I., 41

MRM (multidimensional Rasch model), 37

Multidimensional 2-parameter logistic (M2PL) model, 31–34

Multidimensional 3-parameter
   logistic (M3PL) model,
   34–35
Multidimensional 4-parameter
   logistic (M4PL) model,
   35–36
Multidimensional extension of the
   generalized partial credit
   model (MGPCM), 51–54
Multidimensional graded response
   model (GRM), 47–51
Multidimensional item response
   theory (MIRT), 13–14
Multidimensional latent class
   model, 45
Multidimensional random
   coefficients multinomial logit
   model, 54
Multidimensional Rasch model
   for learning and change, 54
   for repeated item
      administrations, 54
Multidimensional Rasch model
   (MRM)
   compensatory MIRT models, 37
Multidimensional Rasch partial
   credit model, 54
Multilevel IRT models for nested
   data, and MIRT application,
   113
Muraki, E., 61, 66
Muthén, B., 89

Nonparametric MIRT models, 113
Nonparametric models, 17

Partially compensatory MIRT
   models, 38–41
Person parameters in MIRT, and
   descriptive MIRT statistics,
   67–70
Polynomial models, 17

Polytomous data models
   difference models, 14–15
   divide-by-total models, 15–16
   graded response model (GRM),
      14, 15
Polytomous MIRT descriptives,
   and descriptive MIRT
   statistics, 71–74
Porcu, M., 52
Pretz, C. R., 37

Quantitative Applications in the
   Social Sciences (QASS)
   series, 1–2

Rasch model. *See also* Multidimen-
   sional Rasch model (MRM)
   about, 26
   UIRT estimation methods, 26
R code
   dichotomous data in MIRT
      models, 37–38, 41, 45
   estimation in MIRT models, 91
   item factor structures, 82
   MIRT application, 107,
      109, 111
   polytomous data in MIRT
      models, 54
   unidimensional item response
      theory (UIRT), 13,
      17, 26
Reckase, M. D., 75, 80, 110
Reise, S. P., 81
Resources, for MIRT
   application, 113
Revuelta, J., 54, 90
Rizopoulos, D., 41
Rodriguez, A., 81

Sam, K. L., 37
Samejima, F., 14
Schilling, S., 88, 89

Scoring, and estimation methods, 24–26
Sinharay, S., 35
Spray, J. A., 42
Squires, J., 52
Stout, W., 93, 95
Sulis, I., 52
Surber, J., 109
Svetina, D., 96

Testlet response model, and item factor structures, 81–82
Test-level fit assessment, and MIRT model diagnostics and evaluation, 97–100
Test-level MIRT descriptives, and descriptive MIRT statistics, 75
θ-space, and descriptive MIRT statistics, 55–56
Thissen, D., 52–53, 84
Thomas, M. L., 81
Toland, M. D., 52
Two-tier model, and item factor structures, 77–80

UIRT (unidimensional item response theory). *See* Estimation methods, and UIRT; Unidimensional item response theory (UIRT)
Unfolding models, 17
Unidimensional item response theory (UIRT). *See also* Estimation methods, and UIRT

about, 2–3, 5
assumptions, 5–6
asymmetric item response functions models, 17
dichotomous data models, 6–13
divide-by-total models, 15–16
latent trait, 5
nonparametric models, 17
polynomial models, 17
polytomous data models, 13–16
R code, 13, 17, 26
unfolding models, 17
unipolar models, 17
Unipolar models, and UIRT, 17

Van Rijn, P. W., 35
Variable compensation models, 42
Von der Embse, N. P., 51

Wainer, H., 81–82
Walker, C. M., 109
Wang, L., 82
Wang, X., 81–82
Way, W. D., 35
Weeks, J. P., 107
Wetzel, E., 52
Wilson, M., 3

Xie, H., 52

Zhang, B., 109
Zhang, J., 1, 93, 95